5 SECRETS TO MULTIPLY YOUR REAL ESTATE PORTFOLIO

NEW INVESTORS GUIDE TO INCREASING YOUR ROI

E.J. WILLIAMS, U.S. ARMY VETERAN

© Copyright 2021 Blackstone Street Publishing LLC - All rights reserved.

It is not legal to reproduce, duplicate, or transmit any part of this document in either electronic means or in printed format. Recording of this publication is strictly prohibited and any storage of this document is not allowed unless with written permission from the publisher except for the use of brief quotations in a book review.

Under no circumstances will any blame or legal responsibility be held against the publisher, or author, for any damages, reparation, or monetary loss due to the information contained within this book. Either directly or indirectly. You are responsible for your own choices, actions, and results.

Legal Notice:

This book is copyright protected. This book is only for personal use. You cannot amend, distribute, sell, use, quote or paraphrase any part, or the content within this book, without the consent of the author or publisher.

Disclaimer Notice:

Please note the information contained within this document is for educational and entertainment purposes only. All effort has been executed to present accurate, up to date, and reliable, complete information. No warranties of any kind are declared or implied. Readers acknowledge that the author is not engaging in the rendering of legal, financial, medical or professional advice. The content within this book has been derived from various sources. Please consult a licensed professional before attempting any techniques outlined in this book.

By reading this document, the reader agrees that under no circumstances is the author responsible for any losses, direct or indirect, which are incurred as a result of the use of the information contained within this document, including, but not limited to, — errors, omissions, or inaccuracies

CONTENTS

Introduction	vii
1. Why Invest in Real Estate? The Basics	1
2. Partner Up!	21
3. Leveraging REITs	41
4. Flip 'em	47
5. Join a Real Estate Investment Group	63
6. Invest in Rental Properties	73
7. Bonus Tip - For Veterans & Active-Duty Service Members	93
8. Real-Estate Moguls - The Success Stories	105
Final Words	117

"Ninety percent of all millionaires become so through owning real estate. More money has been made in real estate than in all industrial investments combined. The wise young man or wage earner of today invests his money in real estate."

ANDREW CARNEGIE, BILLIONAIRE
INDUSTRIALIST

MY GIFT TO YOU!!

Get your Free Property Analysis spreadsheet. This tool will help you figure out if the property is right for you. **What are you waiting for?!!** Start calculating your return on investment (ROI) **Right Now!!**

Free Rental Analysis:
www.EJWilliamsInvesting.com

INTRODUCTION

Real estate investing, compared to other industries, has its own unique blend of characteristics, requirements, quirks, and drawbacks. With those individualities comes a distinctive opportunity for reward. Most of the greatest financial success stories in all of history somehow involve real estate investing. But, is it necessarily an industry for you? Choosing any avenue in life involves understanding what you'll be taking on if you choose to go down that route. This chapter explores some qualities of the real estate investing industry that you may or may not be aware of. There are a million industries out there where you can find a job. There's a college degree for just about everything now. With the advent of the internet, there's really no limit to what trades or businesses you can get involved in. And just like they say with dating, there's something for everyone.

But have you noticed how the workplace and the job market have changed over the years? Getting and keeping a job isn't at all what it used to be. Our grandparents worked more labor-intensive jobs, with little creativity, and college degrees were rare. Then college degrees started becoming more popular and a person's path to the workplace was fairly straightforward: Get a degree, and that degree will get you a

INTRODUCTION

job in that industry (probably a 9-to-5 job). Then as the Millennials have arrived, it's started to seem like college degrees mean nothing anymore because so many people remain jobless after they finish school. This has created a situation where people now are really having to take their career paths and income potential into their own hands. Following a standard path is no longer a guarantee of job security.

Real estate investing is one of few industries that fit this demand for creativity. There is no standard job path for real estate investors. You can come from a highly educated background or a minimal education background. You can come from wealthy parents or poor parents. You can be an investor anywhere you want. There's no one right way to be an investor. You can make your investing career whatever you want it to be. You literally get to do whatever you want to do. How many jobs or industries are there where you get to do that? The creative aspects of being in real estate investing can be seen as either positive or negative. Some of these characteristics will make real estate investing more appealing to you and some might make you run as far as possible in the other direction. At the very least they may give you greater insight into what you can expect as you dive into the real estate investing world.

Investing in real estate is a business that has remained more stable over time, being seen as one of the most lucrative and traditional investments in the financial market. The reasons that make this type of investment a good business is diverse. Normally, investment in the real estate market means the possibility of appreciation and a lot of security, after all, over time, properties maintain their value or tend to increase. You have certainly heard the story of a person who invested in land for a very small price and, over time, the area has increased in value, being sold for a price 10 times higher. Yes, it happens quite often. This all shows that the possibility of having losses when investing in real estate is very low. Are you curious and do you want to know how this investment works to increase your equity? Then continue reading, as we will present many tips in this book!

INTRODUCTION

What is real estate investing & how does it work?

Real estate investment refers to the purchase of real estate for the purpose of making a profit, which differentiates it from people who are looking to own their own home, for example. There are several investment alternatives: purchase for lease (monthly, season), purchase for resale (with the possibility of renovation or construction) and much more. There are several price ranges to choose from; from the most popular buildings to the luxury market, between commercial and residential opportunities. There are people who seek to specialize in a certain profile, while others end up diversifying their investments. The best thing is to find a format that best suits your projects, expectations and needs.

There are two existing types of real estate investment, direct investment (buying a property) and investment in real estate through real estate funds (a group of people who take part in a larger enterprise to invest in the units, such as condominiums and buildings). The direct investment in real estate is the most conventional mode and the best known of the market. It is the format in which the investor simply acquires a property with the purpose of making it profitable in some way. Within direct investment, there are several possible strategies for monetization:

- Buy a property and rent it to obtain the rent.
- Buy in the plant to resell afterwards.

Active management (a modality in which the investor buys a property, carries out a renovation, with many improvements and improvements and, soon after, resells the property for a value higher than the cost of the property + renovation).

As for investment in real estate from real estate funds, it is important, first of all, to understand that a real estate fund concerns a pool of resources from various investors—under the closed condominium model. Thus, the interested investor, through the purchase of quoted shares, becomes a partner in one or more real estate projects.

INTRODUCTION

Got confused? Let's summarize it so that you understand it better. A real estate fund is a meeting of several investors, who pool their financial resources to buy investments, since alone they would not be able to invest. Such an investment can be a bank branch, a commercial building, a hospital, a shopping mall, and even a university, for example.

Real estate is a progressive and attractive industry. The real estate market, which today represents a multi-billion-dollar market, continues to grow and is an integral part of life. In short, we are all aware of the need to have a roof over our heads, whether at home, at work, at our leisure activities, etc., and these roofs are built with certain materials and for a specific purpose. The main factors in understanding the structure of real estate are expressed in the following concepts: economy, risk, and investment.

Conceptually, real estate investing is simple. The goal is to invest money to increase it; thus, in the future, even more, the money will be available. Although all investments involve a degree of risk, the potential profit must cover the amount of risk involved. For example, consider the game of monopoly. To win, you buy properties, you avoid bankruptcy, and you rent to buy even more properties. If only it was that simple! In life, the concept is quite similar, but an error in your investment process can have serious consequences.

Real estate investment experts want people to think that they cannot make money in this business without having someone with deep knowledge to help you. Unfortunately, these people are more concerned with creating their own wealth than helping people actually start investing in real estate. They attack people who are eager to make money by offering training courses, and much more, at a high price. In the event that it looks unrealistic, it most likely is.

Remember that the only people who really benefit from these services are those who offer them and receive their money in exchange for information that is easy to find on their own. Even many real estate investment sites benefit from affiliate links and the sale of information that can be found for free elsewhere. In most cases, you will do

INTRODUCTION

your best to dedicate your time and resources to information gathering and research.

The so-called real estate gurus are on the market to sell your ideas and convince you to invest. They are not interested in teaching you the intricacies of real estate investing. Rather, you have to depend on data; for example, this guide gives the data you need without costing you additional cash. You do not have to spend thousands of dollars on training if you want to start your investments.

If you feel that you would really benefit from the help of a real estate investment professional, do your own background research and look for online reviews on third-party sites. This information will allow you to make a wise choice and not be fooled by a scammer. As long as you are not trapped in big promises, you can find the support you need to make real estate investing a profitable opportunity for your future.

I have developed this book to guide you through the basics of real estate investing and help you make the right choices so that you can capitalize on real estate investing for a financially healthy future. It will provide you with a basic understanding to assist you in getting started from a professional and personal point of view.

1
WHY INVEST IN REAL ESTATE? THE BASICS

INVESTING in real estate usually means that your goal is to have money both now and in the future. This is a great way to ensure that there will be money in your future once you have gotten your investments up and running properly. When set up properly, you will be making enough profit to be able to cover the risks that you are taking in purchasing new houses to rent out or sell as well as the cost of owning the property like the insurance, utilities, and other necessities. Once you understand the basics, you will be able to invest and make it as easy as playing a game of monopoly with your family. Before we begin to discuss some of the benefits of having real estate investments, it is important that you know that real estate is considered to be an alternative investment class all together. When you begin to invest in real estate, you will have a portfolio that will show all of what you have done as far as your investments go. Your portfolio will have several different qualities that will be able to enhance the return with a larger portfolio or even be able to reduce your portfolio risk on the same level of return.

Real estate historically has been a safe, sound, solid investment. It tends to go up in value, provides cash flow from rental income and offers tax benefits and incentives. Over time equity value increases as your loan is paid down. Are you certain that real estate investing is right for you? Do you have a powerful and motivating 'why' that will drive you to succeed? Are you confident you now know how to think like a successful investor? Now you are ready for the right real estate education. When the student is ready, the teacher appears. Real estate investing encompasses a vast ocean of information that can be very intimidating and extremely difficult to consume all at the same time. The goal of this section is to simplify the many different facets of real estate investing and to show you how to understand such a large topic quickly and easily.

To use a fishing analogy, when trout fishermen are trying to assess where the fish are located on a very wide river, they separate the wide river into many small streams. Some parts of the river may be fast and shallow while others slow and deep. Whereas looking at a very wide river can be very intimidating and confusing, when mentally separated into several small streams, evaluating the river and finding the fish becomes much easier. We're going to take that same approach here and segment real estate investing so that it is much easier for you to understand the different facets, starting with the simplest segmentation of all. The purpose of investing in real estate is to make money and you make money in real estate either now or later. Therefore, real estate investing can be summarized into two groups: fast cash techniques and wealth building strategies.

Fast cash, or making money now, provides you with cash in your pocket. For many people, extra money is very important to them right now. Wealth accumulation, or making money later, may provide cash flow and/or a big chunk of cash years into the future, which also has its own benefits. Most notably, making money later in real estate is usually very tax friendly. The IRS has enacted numerous provisions that can reduce the tax liabilities of cash later real estate profits. Also, with some real estate investments you can force appreciation by making improvements to the property, improvements to management, and operations and through upgrades and renovation.

A very important question to ask yourself is, "What do I want out of real estate?" If you are overflowing with liquid assets (cash) right now, either in a retirement account, an inheritance, a business you just sold or simply the steady accumulation of money overtime in a bank account, the prospects of having that money working for you in real estate in a very tax friendly way may be exactly what you want. If you are in desperate need of cash right now, maybe to stay afloat or to pay pressing bills, fast cash may be the smartest course of action for you. In some cases, you may be in the middle of those two extremes and would like both, fast cash and wealth accumulation. Real estate can provide cash now, cash later, or both.

The purpose of real estate investing is to create financial returns, plain and simple. Can your investing actions help people? Certainly! In fact, the way we teach investing is to always do deals that benefit all parties involved. Therefore, it should be a given that when you complete a transaction and make money, you are helping all parties involved. The problem is that sometimes people get so caught up in doing, doing, doing, that they forget to make a profit. Sounds silly, doesn't it? It happens quite often. Whether you are going to make cash now, cash later or both, the purpose of real estate investing is to produce profits (this already assumes that every deal you do is a win-win-win.) Don't allow yourself to fall into the trap of being very active but producing very little economic results.

Now, having real estate investments in your portfolio is a major benefit to you and here are some of those benefits:

1. **Ability to influence performance:** Real estate investment is a tangible asset. Because of this, you can do things that are going to increase the value of the property or even increase the performance of the house when it comes to if people are going to want to rent it or buy it. These can be done by simply fixing a roof that may be leaking, or even repainting the exterior of the house to make it look better instead of having paint chipping off of it. If you have apartment buildings, then you can try and put a higher quality of tenant in the building in order to try and attract other higher quality tenants. As the investor, you are going to have the control of the performance of the real estate that you have invested in.
2. **Diversification value:** This is one of the more positive aspects of having some diversity in your portfolio as far as your asset allocations are concerned. When the returns have low correlations with any other asset class, which will ultimately add to the diversification in your portfolio.
3. **Inflation hedge:** The return of the real estate is tied directly to the rent that you are going to receive from any tenants. There are some leases that will cause rent to increase due to inflation. Then, there are other cases that will cause rent to increase when the lease expires and the tenant resigns the new lease. In both cases, you're going to see the income increase faster in inflationary environments thus allowing for the investor to maintain the real returns.
4. **Yield enhancement:** Real estate will allow for you to achieve a higher return depending on the level of portfolio risk. On the other hand, you may be able to decrease your portfolio risk by maintaining your returns.

There are many reasons why investing in income-producing real estate is a smart way to achieve financial security.

Here are a few.

Profits Through Leverage

With the stock market averaging over eight percent returns annually and real estate growing at an average of five or six percent, to the layman it would appear that the stock market is the better place to invest. This would be true if we were only talking about the appreciation in value from either investment path. However, when coupled with cash flow from rental income and the power of leverage, we are talking about an entirely different scale of success with real estate. With the power of leverage, you can make your money work smarter for you. You can use other people's money (OPM) to help make yourself richer. In the stock market, you cannot leverage your money (except via margins which is an extremely risky investment strategy), but in real estate you can.

Leverage is a very specific and important concept in real estate investment. You may have heard about a rich uncle who just bought a house in cash without taking on any loans. Wouldn't it be great if we all had the resources to do such a thing? Fortunately, purchasing real estate with cash is not a productive use of your money from a financial perspective. The reason is the power of leverage. Leverage can work for most investment methods, but lends itself especially well for real estate investments, since property prices do not fluctuate as drastically as some other types of investments, such as stocks.

So just what is leverage? Essentially, it is the ability to use a little money to buy a big asset. You "leverage" a small percentage of money and personal risk into buying a larger asset. In real estate, you typically put down 20% of the sales price as your down payment. However, with proper planning you can put as little as 10%, 5%, or even no money down. Then typically a bank (or the seller) would lend you the rest of the money to purchase the property. So, you would be using other people's money (OPM) to buy a valuable asset.

The advantages of using leverage are twofold.

First, because more money is invested, leverage significantly increases the percentage of profit you can make. Second, and more importantly, leverage allows you to purchase a much larger investment than you would normally have been able to. To better understand the power of leverage, let's compare the stock market against a similar initial dollar real estate investment.

Relative Safety

Investing in real estate is one of the safest investments you can make. Unlike stocks or funds, you have a great deal of control over the profitability of your investment. For instance, you get to make the choices of the property and you can take an active role in the management. You have a tangible asset with real value. Further, unlike investing in stocks, you choose and control your return on investment. Given the volatile nature of business investing, specifically in light of so many recent corporate scandals the benefits of real estate investing become very clear.

Another benefit is the overall control you have in real estate. If you ever feel as if you are taking a big risk, you may want to take a step back and evaluate your end needs and aggressiveness. The biggest thing you can do to reduce your risk is to keep a high reserve. If you only buy properties with positive cash flow and you keep six to twelve months of expense reserves available, nearly nothing can happen that will cause you to lose your investment.

There are many other ways you can protect your investments. You can conduct thorough market research and do your due diligence on the property. Also, you can purchase your property with a larger down payment, which in turn will reduce your monthly payments, and therefore, your risk. Personally, I would rather use a smaller down payment and keep a larger reserve, but ultimately, the decision is yours to make based on your own comfort level.

Tax Benefits of Depreciation and 1031 Exchanges

You always hear about loopholes for the rich people. Many of these "loopholes" were put into the tax code on purpose to entice Americans to invest in real estate. The tax benefits of owning real estate are tremendous. The two largest benefits are depreciation and 1031 exchanges. With these two tools, you can effectively defer income taxes on a significant portion of your income for a lifetime. Not all the income that you make from your monthly cash flow will be taxable in the current year. This is true because even though the property is appreciating, the IRS will allow you to depreciate a part of your building, which counts as a "paper loss." This is a loss which has occurred but has not yet been realized through a transaction, such as a stock that has fallen in value but is still being held.

For example, let's say you purchase an investment home for $200,000, of which $50,000 of the price is due to the land and $150,000 is due to the dwelling. At the end of the year, you have made $20,000 in gross rental income. You can deduct all your expenses (except mortgage pay down) associated with the property. Let us say your expenses were $15,000; if so, your cash flow income was $5,000. This is real income that you place in your pocket. However, the government will allow you to depreciate the dwelling over its useful life (usually 29 years) and therefore would allow you to depreciate about $5,000 from the building. This depreciation is a paper loss, and is added to your expenses. Therefore, your net income for tax purposes is zero, and therefore you will not owe any money. This depreciation write-off is one of the biggest benefits of owning real estate.

Additionally, if your property did not produce positive cash flow, up to $25,000 per year of loss can be written off your earned income. I hope that if you needed to use this loophole it would not represent a real loss, just a loss after depreciation. To be able to take the $25,000 loss off your W2 salary, you must maintain an active role in the property. The second biggest benefit is when you're ready to sell the property and purchase a larger property. You can complete a 1031 tax deferred exchange of the property (it gets its name from Section 1031 of the U.S. Internal Revenue Code), also called a Starker exchange, named after a man who successfully convinced the courts that based on the exchange of real estate, no tax was immediately due.

This exchange allows you to sell your existing property, place the proceeds with a designated intermediary, and then purchase the larger property. Providing you do not take any cash out of the transaction, it's a tax-deferred event, meaning you will not have to pay taxes on the proceeds until you sell the "upleg," or the replacement property purchased in a 1031 exchange, so called because typically the taxpayer trades up in an exchange. Even then, you can defer the taxes on the sale once more by completing another 1031 exchange.

Be aware, there are several criteria that you must meet in order to complete a 1031 exchange. Some of them include the upleg property must cost more than the sales price of the property you are selling, the mortgage on the upleg must be higher, the transaction must be handled by an intermediary, and you must identify and purchase the upleg property within a designated time frame. After you complete the upleg, you can refinance to pull out cash. You should not refinance before completing the transaction, since the IRS has ruled that these funds would be taxable. As with any tax issue, you should consult your accountant for advice on both depreciation and 1031 exchanges. However, this section should at least give you the basis to start an informed discussion and if necessary, further research into the subject.

Property Management Makes It Easy

It is recommended that you self-manage your properties for at least the first year or two. You will only have a couple of properties, so they should be manageable. This way, you can get the inside experience on what it takes to rent, manage, and complete maintenance on a property. You may find it harder or easier than expected. As a real estate investor, property management is a vital part of your success. After you have purchased ten or twenty properties, you will not be able to grow more if you do not hire professional property management. The reason for this is simple: As you will have learned, overseeing the daily operation of your properties is time consuming. Toilets never clog when the time is right for you, as such disasters always seem to occur on a Sunday morning or during a family birthday party.

On top of that, there are some things that you may want to think about when you are getting into real estate investing. These conditions require special considerations in any of your investment decisions.

1. **Difficult to acquire:** You may find it challenging to build a diversified and meaningful real estate portfolio. Make sure that you make purchases in a variety of geographical locations and

in different asset classes so that you can reach out to many different investors. However, you can also purchase units in the private pool or public security. You'll find that these units are most likely going to be backed by a diverse portfolio.

2. **Costly to buy, sell, and operate:** When you're making a purchase on the private real estate market, your transaction costs are going to be different than those in other investment classes. It is more efficient to purchase larger real estate assets because you're going to be able to spread the cost over a larger asset base. You'll find that real estate is costlier to operate being that it is tangible and is going to require ongoing maintenance work.

3. **Requires management:** There are very few exceptions to this. Most real estate is going to require management on two different levels. The first is going to be the property management. This position is going to deal with all the day to day operations on the property in order to make sure that everything is going properly. The second level is going to be strategic management of the property in order to consider the longer-term market position of your investment. There are times that the management functions are combined and handled by one group. But, remember that management is going to come at a cost; even if you are handling it yourself because of the time and resources required to keep the property up.

4. **Leasing market (Cyclical):** Just like other asset classes, you'll find that real estate is cyclical. Real estate also has two different cycles: the leasing cycle and the investment market cycle. The leasing market is going to be the market for space in real estate properties. Just like many markets, the conditions are going to be dictated by supply and amount of space available as well as demand. Should the demand for space increase, the space available will decrease. As soon as rent is able to reach economic levels, developers will be able to construct additional spaces in order to meet the demand.

5. **Investment cycle (Cyclical):** On the demand side of the investment market is going to be when the investors are going to have capital in order to invest in real estate. You'll notice that the supply side is going to be where all the properties are bought in order to be marketed by their owners. Should the supply of capital that is seeking real estate investments is plentiful, then you'll notice an increase in property prices. As the prices increase, then more properties are going to be bought in order to meet the demand.

The Real Estate Market Cycle:

Tipping point: Prices fall, compensation for the over-building as well as the high prices. Foreclosures will begin to rise because homeowners cannot sell due to owing more than their home is worth.

The decline: Prices will continue to fall and foreclosures are going to flood the market. People are not going to want to buy which will cause there to be more inventory and prices to continue to fall.

The bottom: Prices will bottom out and investors will begin to purchase an excess of the inventory. The deals are going to be plentiful and the cash flow will be at an all-time high.

The climb: Home buyers will grow more confident which will lead to more sales and a decrease in the inventory as well as higher prices.

The peak: Prices are going to be at an all-time high and inventory will be low. You will most likely have multiple offers and may end up selling above asking price.

Investing in real estate has become more popular during the last fifty years and is considered to be one of the most important investment vehicles. Even though the real estate market has numerous opportunities for making money, purchasing, and owning real estate, this is more complicated than simply investing in stocks or bonds.

Basic rental properties

This is one of the oldest real estate investment practices. It involves someone purchasing property and then renting it to tenants. Owners are responsible for paying mortgages and costs associated with maintaining the property. Landlords can charge extra to cover aforementioned costs and to produce a profit for themselves. Furthermore, the property can be appreciated in terms of value.

A main difference between rental properties and other investment types is the time and work spent on maintaining the investment. When you purchase a stock, it's going to stay in your investing accounting and increase in value.

Real estate investment groups

Real estate investment groups are similar to mutual funds for rental properties and are the perfect choice for you if you aren't looking for the hassle of taking responsibility as landlords. An example of this would be purchasing apartment blocks and then enabling investors to purchase them through the company, therefore joining investment groups. Single investors are able to own numerous or one complex. In exchange for this type of management, the company is going to be able to take a part of the monthly rent. Even though this is definitely a safe way to enter the real estate investment sector, many groups are susceptible to the exact fees that trouble the mutual fund sector.

Real Estate Trading

This is considered to be real estate's wild side. Real estate traders purchase properties with the purpose of holding them for a specific amount of time, often not more than four months, hoping to sell them in return for a profit. This technique is known as flipping properties as well and depends on purchasing properties that are undervalued or in hot markets. Pure property filters aren't just going to put money in real estate for enhancements where the investment needs to have intrinsic values, so it can gain profit without any alteration or they won't even take it into consideration. Flipping in this way is considered to be a short-term investment. If property fillers become caught in situations where they can't unload properties, this can be overwhelming, as these investors don't maintain enough cash—so they can pay mortgages on long term properties. This can result in continued losses for real estate traders who are not able to offload real estate in poor performing markets.

REITs

An interesting fact is that real estate has been in the world since our ancestors, so it isn't surprising that Wall Street was successful in finding a way to transform real estate into an instrument that is publicly traded. Real estate investment trusts (REIT) are created when an organization (or the trust) utilizes the money of investors to operate and buy income properties. REITs are purchased and sold on major types of exchanges, like other types of stocks. Companies have to pay 90% of their taxable profits in the type of dividends, to maintain its position as a REIT.

Getting Started with No Cash, Really?

It may seem like you would need money to invest in real estate. After all, you cannot do a real estate transaction without it. Where does this money come from? That's the difference. You do not need your own money to start investing in real estate, but you need to find a source of financing. However, when you plan to invest with other people's money, it is essential to learn how to sell yourself and give others the assurance that you can also help them make money.

If you do not have money to invest and want to present your idea to other stockholders, you need to determine what you can bring to the table. Maybe you have experience in real estate, or you have the relationships needed to make intelligent real estate transactions. It may be time to look for the right properties at the lowest price. Whatever you have to offer, you must convince your supporters to trust you with their money. When you do not have your own money, you will need to find funds from other sources, such as:

- Partnerships
- Low-repayment loans
- VA or no down payment loan
- Wholesaling
- Lease Option Strategies
- Direct purchase from sellers
- Private financing
- Real estate loans or other lines of credit

We will discuss each of these options later in this Real Estate Investment Guide. The crucial thing to be aware of here is that, yes, you can invest in real estate without having money to finance you. However, it is not at all times, an easy path. It requires diligence, creative thinking, and trust.

How to make money in real estate without investing

Investing is not the only way to make money in real estate. If you cannot get the funds to start investing or if you want a different approach, there are many lucrative career opportunities on the ground. Among them are:

- Mortgage brokers
- Real estate brokers / agents
- Real estate assistants
- Resident managers
- Real estate managers
- Evaluators
- Title / Escrow Agents

Embarking on one of these career fields can be a great option to connect and prepare for the world of real estate investing. You will gain valuable experience and be an asset when you are ready to start your investment projects.

Real Estate Investing Does Not Imply A Fast Money Quick Scheme

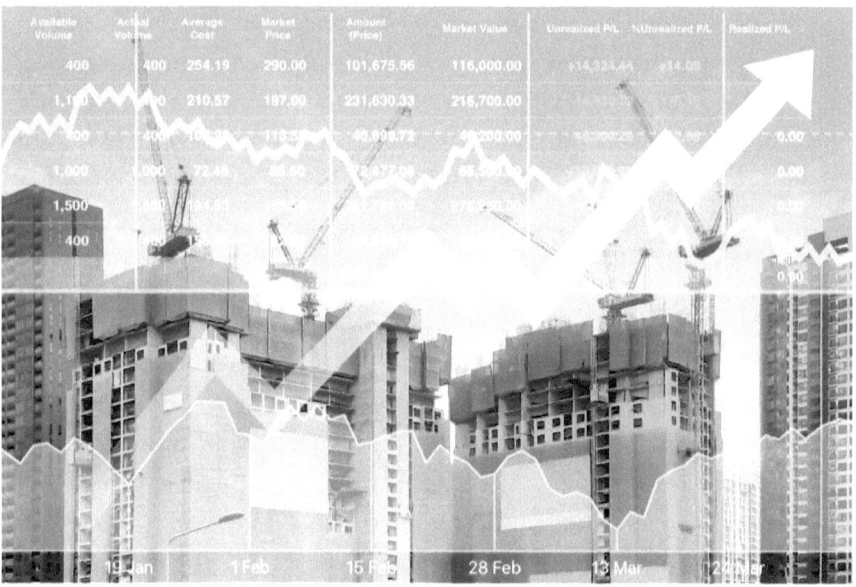

Nearly half of new investors never go beyond their first year. The reason is not lack of knowledge or even agreements, but because they think that business is easier than it really is. Excess stocks of real estate launched on television clearly show what investment activities are. If you look at these programs, it seems that all you have to do is find a property that you like, work and wait 45 days for the buyer to appear. Everyone in business knows that it is far from the truth. More importantly, real estate investing is not a way to get rich quickly. It takes a lot of dedication and hard work.

There are pitfalls in almost every area of activity. Even in the best conditions with the best of times, it still takes months to buy and sell a house. Wholesaling can be done much faster, but it will not produce the returns sought by many new investors. In the end, after paying all the expenses and all the obligations, the end result of each negotiation may make the new investors less excited. They think they will succeed in every business, but the reality is that most real estate investments involve getting single and double investments and waiting for the right opportunity to energize them.

The returns of each company may be lower than expected, and the work much larger than expected. That's how the investment is made. If you think it will work in six months and there will be a dozen fences and a net worth of $ 1 million, you are not in the real world. Real estate business can be very lucrative, but like any other business, it takes time and a lot of work to develop. If you do not see instant results, it can be easy to think that the company is not for you or that you do not have a passion for succeeding.

It usually takes years before a night's success is successful. Many investors have been in business for years until they find a niche or contact that will help them grow. The idea of doing more than one market than you would for a year at your previous job is appealing, but that's not the norm. The reality is that you may have to hit the sidewalk or spend some time running a direct mail campaign. You can deal with 10 owners just to leave with a possible deal. They do not show it on television, but that's where your business is. Even after reaching this point, you still have to deal with the rehab costs, budget, and problems of the buyer before closing. There is a great opportunity to invest, but it does not happen without a lot of work and perseverance.

If you have a real passion for real estate, you can succeed in a much shorter time, but even that will not happen in the first 30 days. There is no magic formula or rapid enrichment in real estate. Investing has always been about working hard and educating, despite what you can see on TV.

What You Should Expect in The Real Estate Business

Most people make the mistake of expecting everything to turn out as easy as they may have thought. It is not the case with real estate businesses. They are faced with a lot of competition, and you need to keep your business up to be the best. You need to invest in your business and strive to make it unique as much as possible to remain relevant. If you are willing to learn and sacrifice, you will surely get excellent results.

Not an easy task

Starting the real estate business may not be that rosy at first, as it will take a toll on your time and sleep, thinking about the best ways to grow and improve your businesses. You might need to research a lot on the market, the property's location, the gents you will use to get clients, and so on. To ensure everything is going on smoothly, it will take a lot of hard work, determination, and sacrifice. Success and profits will not come on quickly. It takes time and perseverance. You should not be faint-hearted if you need to experience success. Always keep in mind the idea that you have crossed the battle line, and you have to do everything it takes to emerge the winner.

Be creative

For any real estate business, you should expect to be more open to ideas. Learning new things and solving the challenges in the real world will help you grow your business. As much as you have the knowledge and expertise in your profession, it will take more than that to come up with the right decision to help you grow. You do not have to rely on your family and friends to help you solve your work issues. Being your boss comes with many responsibilities that need you to be reliable and go beyond your comfort zone to see you grow into a successful real estate agent. You will learn how to handle your issues peacefully within yourself and use the most innovative and creative ideas to improve your business and make the decisions right for it.

You will need help

When starting your business, you are probably afraid of getting new experiences. At the same time, you may find yourself excited about seeing your business grow. As you may be new in the industry, you may need somewhere to lay your shoulder on. You may have to ask for help with running your business. Most real estate agents use brokers (salespeople who have expertise and experience in negotiating deals). They are an excellent resource for the growth of your business. They will prepare you for what you will meet on the way to your success and how you need to finalize deals or decide on the property value as they have been on the market for long.

Make room for disappointments

Just like any other corporate out there, you have to make room for failures. It may not be that easy to be relevant in the industry within a day. It will entail a lot of time and effort to become somebody. You may feel like giving up at some point in the journey but reminding yourself why you chose to start it in the first place may help you remain firm. You will be disappointed by your team or the tenants you sold or rented a house to. In most situations, the tenants are always hard to handle and want to control you, but getting good takes a miracle. Being prepared for disappointments will save you from heartbreak all the time. You have already prepared your mind for failures once something negative comes about. Readily accepting mistakes and learning from them will significantly help. You can learn to take things easy next time. It's simple and effective once you plan for its possibility. Choosing to ignore and handle issues should keep you going. You can strive to make yourself better.

Profits

Real estate businesses are very popular with successful profits. Once you have mastered the art of convincing your potential clients into buyers, you may have to sit and wait for your bank alert. It takes a lot of time and patience, but once you have a perfect property most people are yearning for, you will quickly sell them. You need to research more on the kind of location that mostly fits a particular type of real estate business and strive to get the best quality properties. Not overpricing will get you more clients. As small the profits may be at first, you can invest them in a more meaningful way to secure your future and save you during tax payment. It is a lucrative business, and it reaps benefits.

You need to grow your business

Once you start a business, you have to look for ways to make it grow. Consider using your knowledge, expertise, and influence to grow the leads and networks. You need to build relationships with people. The more people know you, the more there will be potential buyers. It may not be an easy task, but you need to market yourself. People must know what you are selling or what you are into. Putting yourself out there will significantly help you make the right networks. You can simply connect with your family and friends, attend community gatherings, and use online platforms for marketing you as a brand. However, it may not be simple as you need to sacrifice a lot to get what you are looking for.

Stick to your plan and budget

Once you make plans on how to run the business, you should not dwell on how to get clients while forgetting what you need to do to make a great impression on your business. That being said, your budget should not exceed your ability. You should not forget your needs and invest everything you have in the business. Ensure you have a budget covering all your life areas, not leaving anything behind and sticking to the budget. The more times you add money to the already formed budget, there is a possibility you will have a shortage in other areas. Be disciplined when handling money and not forgetting you and your business needs as well. A good plan will always yield good results. Always being prepared will help a great deal.

Chapter Summary

In this Chapter we learnt about, Why Invest in Real Estate? The Basics:

- Getting Started with No Cash
- Real Estate Investing Does Not Imply A Fast Money Quick Scheme
- What You Should Expect in The Real Estate Business

In the next chapter you will learn about Partnering Up.

2

PARTNER UP!

Partnerships, Limited-Liability Companies, and Subchapter S Corporations

THE MOST POPULAR form of ownership for commercial real estate investments is a partnership (limited partnerships are more common than general, and the term is used in this book to include limited-liability companies that are taxed as partnerships, but not limited-liability companies that have elected to be taxed as associations [i.e., corporations]). A partnership is generally governed by the laws of the state of its formation. A partnership is a legal entity in which two or more entities or individuals agree to cooperate to advance their interests and to share profits or losses. Partnerships are taxed for federal income-tax purposes as "pass-through entities" in which all items of income, loss, gain, and credit are allocated to the partners or members, who then pay income tax themselves. Generally, there is no "second level of federal income tax" at the entity level for partnerships.

This is in contrast to federal income taxation of Subchapter C corporations ("C-Corps"), for which "two levels of federal income tax" are imposed once at the entity level, then again at the shareholder level. The partnership entity (unless it is a single member LLC, in which case it is disregarded for federal income-tax purposes) files an annual tax return on Form 1065, then delivers a Schedule K-1 to each partner or member, which informs the recipient (and the IRS) of the tax attributes for which it must account for in its own Form 1040 income-tax returns. Each member or partner is responsible for paying its own federal income tax for the tax attributes of income, loss, gain, and credit allocated to it, as shown on its Schedule K-1. There must be coordination between a partnership agreement's provisions governing the allocation of tax attributes and those governing the distribution of cash, to ensure that the allocations have "substantial economic effect." Again, a tax lawyer should be consulted early and often in negotiating and drafting any partnership agreement.

A general partnership has two or more general partners, each of which has unlimited liability for the obligations of the property and partnership. For this reason, in general partnerships, the investors often use limited-liability entities, rather than individuals, to serve as the general partners. In most states, a general partnership does not require a state filing to come into existence, though third parties generally require local recordings at the county level, not to form the entity, but to evidence the existence and authority of the general partnership to take whatever action is necessary in a real property transaction. A limited partnership has at least one general partner, again with unlimited liability, and one or more limited partners—which, as the name suggests, have liability that is generally limited to their equity invested in the entity. Most states require a simple filing at the state level to form a limited partnership, and the partners enter into a limited partnership agreement (or a limited-liability company agreement or operating agreement) to set forth the rules of governance. This agreement is not filed with the state or county, or otherwise made public.

(An "LLC") limited-liability company is a flexible type of entity which combines the fundamentals of a partnership and a corporation. It generally provides limited liability to its owners in most states. Like a limited partnership, it is generally formed with the filing of a simple document at the state level, and it must have an agreement to govern its operations (variously named, such as a limited-liability agreement in Delaware or operating agreement in California). In some states, such an agreement may be oral, but that is not a sound practice (for a number of reasons). The primary characteristics that an LLC shares with a corporation are limited liability and unlimited life; in most states, LLCs may have only one owner (which is a "member" rather than a stockholder or shareholder). The primary characteristics that an LLC shares with a partnership are flexibility in management and the availability of pass-through federal income taxation. Unlike, the management of an LLC can be quite informal. It can even be less formal than either a general or limited partnership. Most states allow an LLC to be governed by the members, by a manager who is a member, or by a manager who is not a member. For federal income-tax purposes, a single member LLC is a "disregarded entity" that does not have to file a separate tax return and instead is consolidated with its sole member for federal income-tax purposes. Indeed, the disregarded single-member LLC should not even have its own federal taxpayer ID number but should instead use that of its sole member. Under federal income-tax law, an LLC will be taxed as a partnership, unless it affirmatively files a form to be taxed as an association (i.e., corporation).

While state law must be consulted for any entity, the state law variations for LLCs are greater than for any other entity. Most states permit single-member LLCs. Most states follow federal income-tax law as to whether the entity is a "pass-through entity," but some differ as to what income-tax deductions are allowed. Some states impose "fees" on the LLC as an entity (which, in practice, are like taxes). For example, in California, a California domestic LLC, or an LLC formed in another state that is qualified to do business in California as a foreign LLC, must (in addition to its annual franchise tax) pay a fee on its total income over $250,000 per year, on a graduated basis, up to $12,590 (as of August 2017). Some investors seek to avoid the fee by using a limited partnership, but the additional expense and complexity, and the relatively small upper limit of the fee, lead most investors to proceed with an LLC.

Most sophisticated investors form their LLCs in Delaware, then register them as foreign LLCs in the state or commonwealth in which the property is located. There are a number of reasons for this. The Delaware Secretary of State's office is far more efficient than those of most other states. The Delaware law governing LLCs is among the most flexible, especially as it relates to the modification of fiduciary duties of care and loyalty. Delaware's Court of Chancery is viewed as the preeminent medium for the resolving of disputes that involve the internal matters of LLCs, and it has an established body of common law to interpret, or to fill in any gaps in, statutory language. Perhaps most importantly, lenders (especially conduit lenders) and institutional investors are more comfortable with Delaware entities.

Subchapter S Corporations ("S-Corps") are small business corporations with limited liability, similar to regular C-corporations. Under the federal income-tax code, a number of requirements must be satisfied to permit a corporation to qualify to elect Subchapter S status, such as limitations on the number of shareholders and other formalities. An S-Corp must also adhere to state law corporate formalities for corporations, such as having bylaws, a board of directors, officers, and meetings that are noticed and held as required by state law. While S-Corps are generally pass-through entities, like partnerships, for federal income-tax purposes, the income-tax laws of the states differ. For example, California does impose an income tax on S-Corps at the entity level but at a lesser rate than for a C-Corp. Thus, in California, a shareholder in an S-Corp would incur (i) only one level of federal income tax, at the shareholder level, and (ii) some state income tax at the entity level, plus state income tax at the shareholder level.

S-Corps are generally not used to hold commercial real estate assets, mainly because of limitations on income-tax deductions that the shareholder may otherwise use. For example, in a partnership, each of the partners is generally able to deduct its share of interest on the amount of the debt secured by a lien on the property and depreciation on the full value of improvements to the property (even though the acquisition was financed in large part with debt). *1.* Generally, a shareholder in the same situation may not deduct aggregate amounts in excess of its adjusted basis in its stock of the corporation. This limitation on deductions virtually eliminates the use of S-Corps to hold real estate for most domestic US taxpayers.

For these reasons, partnerships are generally used to hold commercial real estate, with state law determining the better choice between a limited partnership and an LLC taxed as a partnership. If a limited partnership is used, the general partner is usually a single-purpose, limited-liability entity. Some investors also use single-purpose entities to serve as limited partners in limited partnerships or managers (or even members) in LLCs. That said, many limited partners in partnerships and members or managers in LLC are willing to forego a second liability shield in favor of the cost and complexity savings in using only a single entity—provided that the limited partnership agreement; or LLC agreement; or operating agreement sufficiently contractually limits rights of members and managers or partners against each other. The entity's liability shield protects the investor against claims of most third parties, while the contractual limits on liabilities protects the investor against claims of the other investors within the entity. With respect to liability to third parties, investors should be aware that there are exceptions to the limited liability that entities can provide. For example, the liability shield applies to limited partners or members only with respect to partnership or LLC obligations to third parties. It does not apply to liabilities that an investor may incur for its own tortious actions.

Most individual real estate projects are structured as partnerships (usually LLCs). Programmatic investments can be structured as programmatic partnerships, funds of various types, or publicly traded or no publicly traded REITs.

Commingled and Separate Account Funds

Many capital market transactions are made using commingled funds (funds that include many primarily institutional investors), or on behalf of a separate account client. The capital source generally retains an investment manager to manage the separate account or sponsor the commingled funds. These investments generally utilize the entity types discussed above, but they may be "mixed and matched" depending upon the type of investor whose money is being put to work. The commingled fund structure can be used for smaller funds or for funds designed to offer interests at "the retail level," through registered broker dealers. These structures can also be used for more complicated investment structures for institutional separate account or commingled fund investors. The additional complexities generally result from the more complex tax and ERISA requirements of institutional investors or the size of the account or fund.

How Do Real Estate Limited Partnerships (RELP) Work?

RELPs offer a twist on basic real estate investment groups. Not only is the legal structure of the deal different, the investment itself is different in character. Here, you own a percentage of a project rather than a discrete unit. RELPS are often created by real estate developers looking for financing for large projects (like building a subdivision). This money is used for new construction or major renovation of existing properties, and the property usually does not generate revenue before the project is completed.

What an Investor or Partner Can Bring to Your Deal

Depending on what you need to make this deal happen, you should look for active partners at the syndicator level (or management level) that can complement what you are bringing to the table. Defining the role of each partner and their contribution is a critical element of any effective partnership. There are several things that an investor or partner can bring to the table to help with the deal:

- They can bring money

- They could have the skills to help you work out the deal

- They can bring mentorship and expertise

- They can bring a track record

- They can bring credibility

- They can be a sponsor or loan guarantor for you if you're new (I will explain more later)

You are looking for partners that can bring one or more of the aforementioned items to the deal. Enthusiasm, desire, and ideas may be nice, but they should not be the strongest suit your partner holds. There is a lot of risk in any transaction.

. . .

Active Partners

Active partners will have an active interest in the management of your group and investment properties. This may include overseeing the management of the property and tenants. It may also include financial or equity contributions that can help you obtain bank financing. An active partner will usually be involved in all major decisions regarding the investment.

You will always be an active partner. That being said, you can work with other active partners that can enhance your access to institutional financing, find more deals and/or enhance your ability to attract investors. All such partners will be decision-makers.

If you have a partner, you will form a separate "management-level" limited liability company to serve as a limited liability company manager or general partner in your group. Your management level LLC will earn the syndicator's equity and fees that can be shared with its members.

In the event that your valued financial backer or accomplice likewise be answerable for a portion of the undertakings related with an arrangement, ensure their assignments are unmistakably portrayed in the administration level working understanding. If your management level joint venture partners will also contribute capital, they should invest alongside your investors so their investment will receive the same return as the passive equity investors. In addition, as a member of the management level LLC, they will receive a portion of that LLC's earnings (equity distributions and fees).

Passive Investors

Passive investors may share in profits (equity investors) or may earn a fixed return on their investment (debt investors). Either may invest in your LLC or syndicate. Passive investors will not share in any of the day-to-day management decisions or property operations. Their duties are limited to providing capital for the purchase and acquisition costs.

Many investors prefer to be passive. They do not want the burden of management, but they do want to benefit from earning a better return on their money than is perhaps offered through other investment opportunities.

Remember that partners and investors, including passive ones, may also be able to provide valuable advice and mentorship in addition to their financial backing. They may have an extensive network or a strong credibility factor that they can use to strengthen your offer.

Here are some things to consider when you are seeking passive investors:

- Offer better returns if they will offer more funds
- Offer better returns if they will invest for longer
- Offer better returns if they allow the payments to accrue
- Offer better returns if they invest early

Passive Equity Investors

Passive equity investors invest money to acquire a percentage of the company you form to take title to real estate (your syndicate). Your equity investors will own a proportionate share of the equity in the investment. Because of their equity stake, they will be included in both the profits and the losses that the property generates, so you will have to account for them.

In exchange for their equity investment, the equity investor will receive a portion of the cash flow, appreciation, depreciation and other tax benefits based on their percentage of equity ownership. You may also structure your deal so that a particular class of equity investors gets a larger share of the tax benefits.

It's important to find out what your investors want when you first start talking about them investing with you. Do they want cash flow, equity or tax benefits? This will prevent you from wasting their time and yours. Doing this in advance of having a deal under contract will help you find and structure deals that are attractive to your investor pool.

Passive Debt Investors

A debt investor in your LLC may offer you their funds in exchange for a fixed return and a return of principal within a specified period of time. The fixed return is treated as a "preferred return," just like what you offered your equity investors. The debt investors get paid first, before the equity investors receive any returns. They get paid immediately after you pay the property operating expenses and any loan payments owed to the bank, if you have a bank loan.

A debt investment may have a shorter duration than your equity investors, requiring a refinance in order to pay them off, and they may require periodic reporting. Your debt investors may have the ability to take over management of the property if you fail to perform as agreed. If you perform as agreed, they simply get paid their money plus a fixed return. Eventually, after they get their principal back, plus the returns you offered, they relinquish their interests in the LLC.

Offering debt interests in an LLC is a useful tool for situations where you have a bank loan that prohibits subordinate debt. It can be used for seller financing in those situations. It can also be used for complex joint ventures with other private equity firms who might invest large sums of money in your deal as a single investor but want a preferred return over your syndicate investors.

Private Lenders

Private lenders will loan you money for your deals in exchange for a specified rate of return or interest rate. You have an obligation to pay back their investment plus interest, and there are usually remedies (such as foreclosure on a property) for default. Look for a person that could loan you money at a 10 to 12% interest rate as a hard money lender. After a few years, they could loan you millions on deals. Though the interest rate is high, that relationship made me millions.

Private lenders fall into two categories:

- Hard money lenders hold themselves out as lender and dictate their terms to you

- Private lenders who are not in the hard money lending business, on the other hand, will accept the terms you offer them

Private lenders offer funds for the purchase or management of the investment. You give them a return of say 5 to 10% on their cash. They do not receive a percentage of the net profits so you don't have to account to them. They do not benefit from loss write-offs. They do not participate in the cash flow. They do not benefit if the equity or property value increases. They simply get paid their money with interest, and eventually, they get their principal back.

Payments on private loans can be made monthly, quarterly, annually, or you can have their interest accrue until a point in the future when the investment is refinanced or sold. Once the debt is paid off, their involvement in the deal is finished.

Their collateral for the loan is generally directly against the property in the form of a promissory note and mortgage or deed of trust (depending on in which state the property is). Private lenders should always be listed as a beneficiary to any property insurance policies. The term, payment schedule, and interest rate are all well-defined in advance.

Which Passive Investor Is Better?

Equity Investors

Pros

- Can participate in all aspects of property ownership
- Receives a return only on what the property generates
- Their investment is not secured by a promissory note

- It does not require payments on their equity deposit like a debt investor
- May require a lower rate of annual return than a debt partner
- Can pool several equity investors together
- Allows you to accept lenders as investors where a bank loan prohibits subordinate debt

Cons

- Have limited voting rights on certain major decisions
- Invests in exchange for an equity position
- Will typically be more expensive, over the long run, than debt investors

Debt Investors

Pros

- Do not participate in profit allocation
- Can be cheaper overall than equity partners
- Can be paid off quite easily. (If there are no prepayment penalties.)
- Can be refinanced out of the deal
- Do not require equity
- Do not receive tax benefit allocations
- Do not receive a percentage of ownership

Cons

- Often require higher fixed returns than equity partners
- May be able to take over control of the investment and put

themselves ahead of your syndicate if you don't perform as agreed
- You must be able to pay off the principal upon maturity, which may be before you sell the investment property

Private Lenders

Pros

Cons

- Do not participate in profit allocation
- Can be cheaper overall than equity partners
- Can be paid off quite easily. (If there are no prepayment penalties.)
- Can be refinanced out of the partnerships
- Do not require equity
- Do not receive tax benefit allocations
- Do not receive a percentage of ownership

Cons

- Often require higher fixed returns than equity partners
- Private Lenders can foreclose on the property if you default on the loan
- You must be able to pay off the loan or principal upon maturity
- You may have required payments along the way, even if there is no cash flow

Limited Partnerships

Limited partnerships are special legal structures created for business purposes. They're made up of at least one general and one limited partner; they can't be the same person, but if there are multiple partners, one person can be both a general and a limited partner. General partners assume all liability for the project and are the only partners that can be directly involved. Limited partners (also called silent partners) put up money for the deal in exchange for ownership shares.

In RELPs, the general partner is usually a real estate developer (or possibly a property management company) who's trying to raise money for a specific project.

How the Money Works

When you invest in a RELP, you hand over a lump sum of money in exchange for an ownership stake in a real estate project or property. Unlike other types of real estate investing, these don't usually provide regular, steady cash flows (though they can). Instead, you get paid back (hopefully more than you put in) when the property gets sold, which can be years later, and the RELP dissolves.

In some cases, there will be preset intervals where investors can cash out portions of their investment. Even with those intervals, though, RELPs are highly illiquid investments and not suitable if you might need quick access to cash.

Pros of A Partnership

There are several professionals to choose from, with whom to partner, including:

Brainstorming - There is some truth to the saying that says two heads are better than one. Someone else can complement your ideas with yours to create a stronger strategy.

More Resources - One person may have limited resources, but if you pool your resources with another investor, you can have a steady acquisition experience.

Analytical Assistance - Analysis is an important part of a successful real estate investment project. Although you are good at analyzing their numbers, someone else can sometimes provide additional information about business performance.

Complementary Strengths - Everyone has their strengths, and it is important to choose a complementary partner to yours. Choosing someone who is exactly like you is usually a bad decision. Look for someone who reinforces your weaknesses to increase your chances of success.

Split Tasks - Depending on the number of investments you plan to make, managing all of this can quickly become a daunting **task.** Teaming up with someone else allows you to divide tasks around how each person stands out and make sure everything is done.

More networking - the network is a part so important in the world of real estate investments. In addition to having someone who can help you in this task, your partners are likely to enter into your partnership with some of their own links that might be helpful to you.

Greater Trust - Real estate investments can be overwhelming, especially for beginners. Working with someone else can help you build your self-confidence and motivate you to move forward.

Reduce your risk - Since you are not the only one interested in the real estate you buy; you reduce your risk of loss. Your partner will absorb some of the losses, just as both will benefit from their success.

Cons of Partnership

Joining a partnership is not the ideal option for everyone. Before you start looking for the ideal candidate, consider these negatives.

Personality issues - Not everyone gets along, which is a normal part of life. Because you will work together and depend on each other for support, it is easy for personality conflicts to bother you.

Differences of opinion - In addition to possible personality conflicts, you can also find differing opinions on important issues. Although some people can solve these problems diplomatically, it can lead to a breakup between you, which can quickly lead to the bankruptcy of your company.

Trust Issues - There is a lot of money involved in real estate investing. If you do not fully trust your partner, you may face serious problems. Trust usually takes a long time to build, and a minor thing can make everything fall apart. Fraud is a serious risk when working with a partner, especially if it is someone you do not know well.

Slow decisions - Some real estate decisions need to be made quickly. However, when working with a person with the same weight, it can sometimes take more than time to make those critical choices and other smaller options.

Reduced profits - Reducing financial risk can be one of the advantages of choosing a partnership, but the coin has another aspect. You will also receive lower profits.

Mix business with pleasure - If you choose someone who is already a friend or you feel that you are getting closer to your part-time partner, it's rarely a good idea to mix friendships with your business. While it's great to have the support of a friend, you can quickly ruin your friendship with bad business.

Unrealistic Expectations - Most people know that they want things to be done and expect everyone else to do the same. In a partnership, this is not always the case. Remember that the other party has their own idea of how things should go. If your partner does not meet your expectations, this can quickly lead to the failure of the partnership.

Responsibilities - When you establish a partnership, you have the same responsibilities as the other party. Essentially, a partnership brings you both together. If someone commits a serious mistake, both will be held responsible. Be sure to ask your real estate lawyer to write a hard contract to make sure nothing is left for interpretation.

Tips for A Successful Partnership

Once you have chosen to join your real estate investment journey, you can follow some tips to ensure a smoother journey:

Commitment - In such a partnership, there will be disagreements. Learn to commit to both being satisfied with the results.

Plan ahead - When you start your new partnership, determine who will handle which tasks, how to handle disagreements, and how benefits will be shared. The more you plan, the more fluid it will be.

Be nice - nobody wants to work with someone who is stubborn and who does not treat her / them well. Be patient and treat your partner with the respect you expect.

Keep communication open - It is important to contact your partner daily. Always stay in touch with the state of daily goals and discuss future projects with your investments.

The bottom line

In terms of partnerships, the benefits are many, but they are not perfect for everyone. Even if you choose not to join a partnership, you do not have to face the real estate investment world for yourself. There are many other investors with whom you can talk to start with yourself and to get referrals. You can also outsource many tasks that you do not have time to complete or skills to manage. Although it will cost money, it allows you to save yourself from sharing your profits right in the middle.

If you choose to find a partner, take precautions right from the start. It can be difficult to find someone you trust enough, but with the right research and someone who shares your goals and ideals, you can develop an effective plan that benefits both. As long as both are committed to making things work, you will be able to achieve great things.

Structuring Your Business Entity

One of the most difficult aspects of starting a real estate investment business, whether it is a partnership or a sole proprietorship, is how to structure it. It is important to protect yourself from personal liability by separating your personal finances from your professional life. In most cases, it is nice to consult a real estate lawyer to review the different options and determine which one is right for you. In California, an "S" corporation or LLC may be better suited to your corporation because they are "pass-thru" tax entities, in which individual shareholders pay a personal income tax. A "C" corporation may be required for more complex organizations—which is a separate taxable entity. In both cases, a real estate lawyer can help you in this decision-making process.

Chapter Summary

In this Chapter we learned Partner Up! covering:

- Partnerships, Limited-Liability Companies, and Subchapter S Corporations
- How Real Estate Limited Partnerships (RELP) Work?
- What an Investor or Partner Can Bring to Your Deal
- Limited Partnerships
- Pros of A Partnership
- Cons of Partnership
- Tips for A Successful Partnership
- Structuring Your Business Entity

In the next chapter you will learn about Leveraging REITs

3

LEVERAGING REITS

Real Estate Investment Trusts

A REAL ESTATE investment trust (REIT) is an entity that has made an effective election pursuant to the Internal Revenue Code that allows it to deduct the amount of dividends that it pays to its owners each year (a "dividends-paid deduction") from income tax that it would otherwise owe. If the REIT distributes to its shareholders an amount equal to all its net operating and capital proceeds (referred to as "funds from operation") for a given tax year, the deductions should eliminate any income on which taxes would be paid at the entity level. This would put the entity in virtually the same position it would have been if it were a pass-through entity (though it is not). In some cases, the dividends that are so paid may be made up in part of REIT stock or other non-cash considerations, subject to certain limitations. REITs can be set up as trusts, corporations, LLCs or, in a few states, an entity actually called a real estate investment trust. REITs are often used in structures known as "UPREITs," in which the REIT serves as the general partner of a limited partnership (known as the "operating partnership," ownership units of which are known as "OP units").

To qualify as a REIT, and to remain a REIT, the entity must comply with a number of technical requirements that go to what types of assets it holds (generally real property, but not "dealer property"), how much of its income qualifies to meet certain thresholds (and falling short of those thresholds because of too much "bad REIT income" is fatal to its REIT status), the amount of dividends that it pays to its owners each year, who the owners are, how concentrated ownership is, how many owners there are, transferability of interests, and a number of other requirements. Generally, REITs must invest in real property assets, but those investments may include either or both of equity investments in real estate (an "Equity REIT") or lender interest under loans secured by real property (a "mortgage REIT"), or both. Generally speaking, rents (other than rents based on net income of the tenant) and interest paid on real estate-secured loans, from third parties, will be "good REIT income." The particular requirements are ever changing and should always be considered with the help of a tax lawyer.

In theory, REITs can be formed under the laws of almost any state or commonwealth, but most are formed in Maryland because the Maryland corporate law was written to work "hand-in-glove" with the REIT tax rules. Maryland also has a wealth of case law on REIT governance, so it provides more certainty as to legal outcomes than other states.

Texas and Delaware also serve as the jurisdiction of formation for many REITs, but no state comes close to Maryland as the "jurisdiction-of-choice" for the formation of REITs.

REITs are not inclined to own operating businesses, and income from operating businesses generally constitutes "bad REIT income." Bad REIT income can be generated in a number of ways, some of which are obvious and some of which are not. Income from amenities and services like parking, gym fees, house cleaning, and the like can be bad REIT income. This issue can affect office or multifamily assets, but it is especially problematic for senior housing, hotels, student housing, and other assets that have an operating business component. The REIT statute provides a structure, within limits, to address these types of assets. In an oversimplified picture, the REIT or its operating partnership acquires the real property asset (nothing else); the business is transferred to a specific type of subsidiary of the REIT (a taxable REIT subsidiary or "TRS"). The TRS acquires most of the assets other than the real property; the REIT or operating partnership, as landlord, leases the real property to the TRS. The TRS enters into a management agreement with a third-party manager who meets certain qualifications; and that manager operates the business using the TRS's leasehold and other assets. The goal is to set the rent under the lease to be close to the amount of operating income the TRS would realize after the manager has paid its own fees and the operating expenses of the business. That way, only the rent is paid to the REIT or operating partnership (as "good REIT income") and the TRS pays tax on whatever income it does not pay in rent. It may be a fiction, but it is a fiction that is widely used.

As mentioned, some REITs are publicly traded entities; some are public, but not traded on exchanges, and some are private REITs used in fund structures (including domestically controlled REITs that are a common tool for offshore investors). Public REITs have a number of advantages that offset the strict rules to which they must adhere. First, the dividends-paid deduction puts the REIT in virtually the same position as a pass-through entity. Second, they provide access to the public markets for equity and debt capital. Third, with the UPREIT structure, they allow the vehicle to acquire properties using a currency other than cash, OP units. "Sellers" of properties to the REIT can take some or all their purchase price as OP units (limited partnership units in the operating partnership) that may be converted into stock of the REIT in the future. So long as the REIT does not sell the property (a matter of some negotiation), the seller does not realize tax until it converts the OP units into shares of the REIT, which allows the seller to defer the gain. An individual OP-unit holder might even avoid income tax altogether by dying, which would cause the holder's basis in its OP units to step-up to fair market value—though this is a drastic step to avoid paying tax. OP units are actually sales of securities (the OP units), so the property acquisition is, itself, a private placement. Any OP unit transaction should be undertaken only with experienced securities and tax lawyers.

As of January 2020, the public REITs' worth market capitalization was trading at $1.4 trillion, per the National Association of Real Estate Investment Trusts and more than 60 private REITs with approximately $95 billion in assets, per Blue Vault Partners, an Atlanta-based research firm. Most of the larger REITs are publicly traded and include such well-known companies as Simon Property Group, Inc., Equity Residential, and Public Storage.

Public REITs trade as common stocks and are owned by individuals, mutual funds, exchange traded funds, and institutions. They provide the benefit of liquidity with daily share pricing, and their net asset value can be determined on a daily basis. REITs can trade at a premium or discount to their net asset value (NAV) depending on the strength of the overall market and private real estate valuations. A number of real estate advisory and consulting firms calculate the NAV of almost all REITs. The NAV of a REIT is the market value of its assets less property liabilities and preferred stock divided by the common shares outstanding to derive a value per share. The market value of a REITs assets is typically calculated using a capitalization rate or a funds from operations (FFO) multiple. The FFO for a REIT is its net income plus depreciation or amortization and plus or minus property gains and losses. Most REITs trade at FFO multiples of fifteen to twenty times. Although REITs are traded as common stocks, they are highly correlated with small cap stocks and, therefore, may not provide portfolio diversification benefits that private real estate equity investment generates.

Chapter Summary

In this chapter we learnt on Leveraging REITs covering the following:

- Real Estate Investment Trusts.
- How REITs is important
- How to use REITs in you investment

In the next chapter you will learn....about property flipping and how it works

4

FLIP 'EM

THE FLIPPING METHOD is purchasing a property that is obsolete and needs work. When the work is done, you trust that the worth of the property has expanded by more than you spent on the upgrades. We should describe a couple of main words. ARV represents After Repair Value. This is the thing that the flipper can sell the house for after it is repaired. Shutting costs are what we, as a landowner, will pay when we are selling a property. Standard commissions to a specialist in private are 5%-6% of the price tag, paid by the individual selling the property. Likewise, we should pay lawful expenses, which we can assess at 1% for this model. Who pays what shutting costs and lawful expenses rely upon what state and district you are in? Every region will have a standard part of what the purchaser pays and what the vender pays, yet this is all debatable in your exchange. A few instances of shutting costs incorporate title search, and exchange charges to pay the lawyer or title organization for their time spent assisting you with purchasing or selling the property.

Recovery financial plan is how much the flipper expects spending on the materials and work (like ledges, new rooftops, new floors, paint, work and grant expenses from the city if pertinent). Contingent upon what sort of condition the house is in and how pleasant you need to make the house will decide how much the recovery spending should be. Holding costs are the costs we must compensate for claiming a property. These expenses incorporate force charges, water charges, property protection, local charges and different costs that accompany property possession. The more you own a property, the more in holding costs you will have. The last piece we need to comprehend is benefit. This is how much the flipper might want to make from the exchange after all costs are paid.

The flipper should purchase the property as per the accompanying recipe:

ARV - shutting costs - recovery financial plan - holding cost - Benefit = Price tag

In the event that a flipper follows the above equation, they will realize the amount to pay for a property when a distributor or specialist comes to them with a potential property they can purchase.

Master Tip: Leave yourself in any event a 30% overall revenue as a flipper. Try not to stop your benefit. In the event that the arrangement doesn't work, it doesn't work. Try not to Twist YOUR Guidelines. Proceed onward to the following arrangement and leave behind managed dainty edges. In the event that you run into surprising costs you didn't get ready for (which you will) you would prefer not to be attempting to flip a house with no benefit for yourself toward the end.

Flipping a house isn't putting resources into land since you are effectively chipping away at an undertaking until it is done. At that point, to make a profit, you need to sell the item. You will possibly bring in cash from a house flip when you effectively offer the property to another person. This is the same as what any item-based business does. They assemble an item, and afterward to bring in cash off of it, they need to sell it. In the event that you don't sell the item, you bring in no cash! With house flipping, the more you hold the house without selling it, the less cash you will benefit on the grounds that your holding costs will rise. This is ordinary business, and it's anything but an awful method to get things done, however we should understand that this is an alternate model and methodology than contributing. Kindly don't mistake flipping for benefits which contribute to long haul abundance and month to month income. At the beginning of your flipping career, you should not aim to do things quickly. You should focus more on getting it done and getting it done the right way so that you will be able to have high-quality homes that people will want to move into once you have finished the project. Once you get comfortable with your investment property skills, you can start trying to move faster to get things done.

Until you sell the home, you are not making any profit. You are only driving yourself further into a loss on the house. It is a problem for many flippers and something you will likely encounter, at least once in your flipping career. You will probably even have a home or two that you do not profit from at all. It is not uncommon for investment properties to be a loss, which cannot be easy to deal with. Don't let it drag you down and try to move onto the subsequent project and do things differently to profit on those. Your reputation as a business person is so crucial in the world of investment properties. It would be best to make sure that people see you as a right flipper and not as someone who rips people off with their completed houses. You could be surprised to find that you will have an easier time selling homes if you have a good reputation than you would if you have continuously ripped people off in the time that you have been in business. Ensure that you have the knowledge of what you are doing when you are renovating the home to save time.

If you have a low reputation in the investment community, you will not sell your houses quickly. People who know you and have seen shoddy work in the past will spread the word around that your flips are terrible and do not do a good job. It is hard to build a good reputation but make sure that you are not creating a bad reputation for yourself in the process. Flippers who have a fantastic reputation in the investment property sector will sell the properties based on their name. If everyone knows your name and knows your work, they will be fighting to buy a home from you. You'll find that people are very interested in the properties you put up, especially if you make sure that you let everyone know that you did the project. The home renovation industry's right name can make a difference and may be the key to your success.

The most important thing to remember when you are flipping houses is that you will get better. You will get more comfortable with the process, your crew, and even selling the home. You may even find that you enjoy taking on many projects at once to help yourself make more money. The more homes you do, the easier it will become. You will someday look back at your first home and wonder how you got to where you are. As a successful investor, you will reap the benefits of flipping many houses quickly and efficiently.

Reflections to Make Prior to Flipping A House

While it may be exciting to think about the repairs that you're to make on your first investment property and what renovations you're going to embark on to improve the value of the home, the reality is that there are plenty of considerations that you need to be making prior to getting to this point. Flipping a home is primarily about allocating your money properly, because if you don't, you're not going to be able to actualize the true value of your investment over the long-term. This chapter is going to look at two factors that you should be considering before you even begin to do any property research. These two topics include the necessity of having a good credit score prior to purchasing an investment property and how much a down payment is going to cost you. Once you understand these two financially-related factors, we can then move onto considerations that are more closely related with actually purchasing a home to flip.

Secrets of Flipping Houses for A Quick Profit

Buying cheap real estate, quickly improving it, and selling it right after it is a proven way to earn money quickly. It is called House turning, and the current economic crisis means that there are several cheap homes that you can buy, and renovate—if you feel you have a knack for D-I-Y repairs and home painting.

Here are several methods to support you get started with flipping homes for quick profit:

Look for real opportunities. Home flipping is all about buying a dirty home—cheaply, doing some cosmetic repairs, and reselling the property for a healthy profit.

If you are unsure whether to buy real estate or not, take someone with you who has experience building and building houses. Otherwise, what you think is a deal could end up costing you a fortune in repairs or even reconstruction. Remember, flipping homes is to spend as little as possible on the renovation.

Make sure that if you plan to go into flipping homes, you get your mortgage pre-approved. This way, you will know what you can afford, and you will negotiate accordingly.

Do your research. If you want to start throwing houses in a particular area, find out what the average prices are, you can buy low and sell at least the average.

When you do the home flipping, you want to do most of the repair and renovation work yourself. This way, you can lessen the expenses and make a bigger profit when you sell. The less you have to hire entrepreneurs, the more money you will earn when you sell.

If you're trying to get into the house by throwing, there are two things you need to avoid like plague-houses with plumbing problems and those with power outages. These are two of the most expensive to solve and will eat into your profits before you know it.

As you can see, there's not much to consider when you start throwing houses. Therefore, if you have some money or can access the financing, you might consider making some extra money from the real estate market as you recover from the recession.

Succeeding in Flipping Houses

Managing to go home and bring big profits is one of the current real estate trends. It means buying a house at a low price or perhaps a neglected house and selling it quickly at higher market value. A successful return of houses can be possible if you give him a lot of effort and follow all the necessary details with this business. To support your needs for you to get started, here are some good tips that would make room for you to succeed in returning homes.

The first thing you want to look at is that you know everything about the house you are buying. You need to see and evaluate what type or type of house is selling quickly, the needs of this particular community, and the average type of house for the average family type. Depending on the destination area, you should also evaluate the average cost of houses in this area. You do not want to overpay this house and make it a longer process for sale.

Many will focus on one problem aesthetically at home, but this is not necessary. It is not what the intuition of being able to launch houses is all about. Keep in mind that houses with aesthetic problems or simply bad houses could work in your real estate niche, but you can return a perfectly beautiful house that is at market price. Faded, dull or fragile colors, tall grasses or ruined gardens, stinky houses, holes on the wall, stains on the carpet, window treatments are just some of the aesthetic problems you are looking for in a home. These aesthetic problems are an easy-to-solve home that can be sold for minimal profit to the succeeding buyer.

Stay away from major renovations like changing the entire roof, major plumbing issues, repairs, great electrical work, wall renovations, and tastes. These are the things you want to avoid. Besides the fact that it will eat your budget, these things take longer to complete because your main goal is to get things moving as fast as possible.

Finally, separating your money from your business money will certainly help you succeed in returning home. The most strategic way is to get a loan to finance the renovation of the house. By following this technique, you will tend to have more control over your budget and avoid mixing up your company finances.

Now that you know some tricks to knock down houses, do your best, do your research, and make sure that you end up with a wonderful job that will bring you profits.

Fixing and Flipping Houses for Profit; How Much to Renovate?

Any investor who wants to make money by returning homes must understand what to repair, renovate, or improve and what to leave alone. It can be a difficult balance. If you improve the house too much, it can be difficult to profit when selling because it is too expensive for the neighborhood. On the other hand, if you improve too little, you may not get the price you wanted because the property's value was not enough to justify your price. Here are some tips to determine the appropriate level of improvement for your home's vibrations.

Your search starts before you even find a property you want. Go to as many open doors as possible in the neighborhoods where you plan to buy. Take a notepad with you and use it to record your observations and ideas. What you are going to do is evaluate the type of services that are typical for the neighborhood. It will let you know what level of renovation you need to apply to your home.

You need to familiarize yourself with the types of features common to most of the best homes. You will gather many ideas to improve your vibration at home and how much money to spend to do it.

Pay attention to the specific parts to see what quality of materials is standard. While renovations should always be quality work, you have plenty of room for maneuver in the types of materials you use. For a modest neighborhood, stick to cheaper (but still quality) floors, suspended ceilings, etc. In some instances, if your home is rich or quickly improves the neighborhood, you can choose several luxurious materials that reflect the potential buyer's more sophisticated tastes.

Ask your realtor what services the most expensive homes that have recently sold in the neighborhood have. Make sure the home you are buying has these features or include them in your home renovation plans.

Always keep your renovations in line with what the buyer expects. It is a mistake to improve your home far beyond the standards of other homes in the neighborhood. The best strategy is to make your house flip just a little better than the most beautiful house recently sold.

Restructuring to avoid

There are some renovations that, as a real estate investor, you don't want to do. They are too expensive and take too much time without a sufficient return on investment. For example, do not buy a house that needs additional measures to par with the neighborhood's most beautiful houses.

If you want to knock down an interior wall to open the space, that's fine. But when you decide to add the house's footprint, you will need a new roof and foundation for additional rooms. For this kind of renovation, you will need architectural plans, engineering plans, permits, and more time and money than it is worth. Stick to home improvements that are simple and cost-effective.

An improvement that adds a special appeal

If you need something to increase your home's perceived value, consider building a wooden bridge in the backyard. A bouquet is relatively inexpensive, but it has a great emotional appeal to the house owner. Bridges are associated with outdoor relaxation and comfort, a fun family barbecue, and other positive events. Most buyers like them. You will find that this feature adds much more value to the home than it costs.

Flipping Houses and Lease-Purchase Agreement

Flipping homes is a good way to make quick money for real estate investors. You need to know some basic concepts and strategies before you start throwing houses and making money out of it. Its study can prevent you from suffering heavy losses that are involved in real estate investments. What are real estate investment and Home launch? Real estate investments and flipping houses are closely related. People involved in real estate investments today make a huge amount of money by throwing houses. Returning homes is simply buying a property and reselling it quickly at higher rates.

It is not difficult for experienced investors to find buyers interested in buying the goods they sell. But if you are a novice, you may encounter some difficulties. Understanding some basic concepts can help you.

- Continuously study your field of market so that you make a fast and profitable business.

- Prepare your finances so that you can conclude the deal profitably.
- Get help from the contract and forms available to assist you in real estate investment and home launch.
- Market your properties and homes you sell, based on your location and market conditions.
- Quickly find the qualified buyer so you can close the deal early.
- Learn all the legal concepts and paperwork involved.

Flipping houses and buying rentals

Renting, buying, or leasing is a great way to attract more buyers to your property. Even if it is more profitable for buyers, it will help you avoid huge losses.

Leasing is a better option to attract buyers who do not have enough money to buy a house. They can take the rental option's help and get from their dream home to rent at home.

They must pay a certain amount of fixed money to the seller as a down payment, and then a fixed monthly rent for the property they use.

Leasing is a contract between buyers and sellers for a fixed time interval. After they have the case, it favors the buyer, and they have the right to buy the house after this period.

Even if the buyer is not interested or finds that it is not a good deal for them, they can return the deal.

Therefore, rental-purchase is a great way by which investors can find interested buyers quickly and easily.

Properly Calculate A Home's After Repair Value

After you've taken the time to figure out what your budget is going to be for your investment property and have also done some research on your current credit score and how you're going to go about getting a loan for the project you're planning to take on, you can finally begin to think about the next step in the investment property process. This chapter is going to focus on a mathematical tool that is perfect to use when calculating and comparing financial information between different properties that you're considering purchasing. This figure is known as the After-Retail Value (ARV). Once you know how to calculate an ARV for any property that you might purchase, you'll be able to easily compare the value of different units, which will make your decision much easier when you finally figure out which property is worth your hard-earned (or hard-borrowed) money.

What is the ARV?

To put it simply, the ARV is the number almost all investment property professionals use when he or she is attempting to figure out how much their property is going to be worth after they've made their desired renovations. Once this figure is calculated, the investor then knows how much profit he or she can expect to see if the home were to be purchased. This calculated number includes the cost of repairs that are going to need to be made on the property, which is why it is a number that most serious property investment professionals find useful if not essential. When you take the time to calculate an ARV for a property in which you're potentially interested in purchasing, you're doing the following for yourself:

1. Figuring out how much money you're going to be spending on the home after you've put down your initial payment and have taken out a loan.
2. Figuring out tentatively how much the home will be worth once you're finished renovating it and have flipped the property
3. Figuring out ultimately whether or not the home in question is worth your money and time.

While you can certainly hire a real estate agent who specializes in house flipping to calculate an ARV for you, if you are looking at a lot of properties during your initial search (and you should be), then it's likely that you're going to want to know how to do these calculations yourself. It's important that you do not underestimate the cost that you're going to accrue by implementing repairs on a property. For example, renovating a kitchen on average is going to cost you between $10,000 to $20,000. A bathroom is most likely going to run you into a similar hole of debt. Tack on other financial considerations such as home-owner's insurance and the cost of making the initial repairs on a home once a home inspector has outlined what needs to be done, and you've got yourself a hefty sum that needs to be added to the initial down payment and cost of the house. This is what calculating an ARV does. It prepares you for the true investment that you're taking on, rather than merely looking at the initial cost of the property.

Factors to Consider when Calculating an ARV:

1. The Housing Market

One of the biggest priorities that you should have as an aspiring investment property owner is doing adequate research on the housing market in which you're interested in purchasing property. If you don't know a lot about the area's housing market in which you're searching, how do you expect to make the smartest and cheapest decisions possible? When you're doing your initial research, it's important that you are gathering information for similar property types. For example, if you know that you want to purchase a multi-family home that contains three units, it will be pretty useless to do preliminary research that includes information on properties that are two-unit dwellings. Another factor to consider involves recognizing any fluctuations in the price of the property over time. For example, if the owner before you made renovations to the property already, you should try to figure out when these renovations were made and how much they cost.

2. Size of the Home

When you're making your initial comparisons, you're going to want to make sure that the size of each home is relatively similar. To do this, check out the square footage of each home and make sure that they are all at least within ten to twenty percent equal to one another.

3. Condition of the Home

When you're thinking about the condition of a particular home, make sure that the home falls within the degree of expectations that you have for your investment property. This should also work within the expectations that you have regarding maintenance cost. If you know that you don't want to spend a ton of money on repair costs, you shouldn't look to purchase a property that needs all new flooring because the previous owner had a cat who didn't know where to urinate. While this example is rather foul, I have personally known investors who have encountered this problem, and to replace the floors ending up costing upwards of twelve-thousand dollars.

After you've thought about *all* of the costs that are associated with the purchase of the property and the cost that it will take to renovate the home in which you're interested, the final step is to calculate the ARV using the following equation:

ARV= [Retail Value*.7]-Rehab

Let's solve this equation through an example. Let's say that you're interested in a property that has a retail value of $250,000. The house is large, but it needs a significant amount of work. After you do some renovation estimating, you find that your renovation costs are going to be around $60,000. Remember, you're going to want to be as detailed as you can be as you make your initial renovation estimates, and it is also probably a good idea to have your estimates be slightly high rather than slightly low. After you do this math, you find that the ARV is $115,000. What this means is that if everything goes as planned, after you're finished renovating the home, the house should be worth around $365,000. Of course, this is largely going to depend on where the house is located and a variety of other factors that need to be considered, but this example should have been able to provide you with a concrete example of ARV in action. The best advice here is to take your time as you do mathematical research for each property that you may end up purchasing, and if you do find that you're unable to adequately do these calculations on your own, it's always safe to find a realtor who can crunch these numbers for you.

Chapter Summary

In this chapter we learnt on Flipping Property:

- Reflections to Make Prior to Flipping A House
- Secrets of Flipping Houses for A Quick Profit

- Succeeding in Flipping Houses
- Fixing and Flipping Houses for Profit; How Much to Renovate?
- How to Properly Calculate A Home's After Repair Value
- Factors to Consider when Calculating an ARV

In the next chapter you will learn....about Joining a Real Estate Investment Group

5

JOIN A REAL ESTATE INVESTMENT GROUP

STARTING AN INVESTMENT CLUB IS A FUN, easy way to learn about investing. It is less risky than investing by yourself, yet just as exciting, as you and co-members increase your financial holdings by pooling funds and investing together on a regular basis. It can also be a fun excuse for a regular social gathering or a way to educate kids about finance. In the realm of real estate investing, it gives you an opportunity to get your feet wet. Now, let it be said, real estate investing is relatively easy to learn, so if you can do it yourself, you should. However, if you are in a situation that limits your educational or financial ability to get started in real estate investing, a small investment group can help you get started.

To start a group, introduce the idea of forming an investment club to people you know who have expressed interest in the real estate market. After a core group of people join up, be sure to immediately agree on common goals for the group. Members who are involved for social or educational reasons may not mix well with serious investors. Next, agree on the level of financial commitment members will make. A large monthly contribution may eliminate members over the long run. Small investments may frustrate investors who want to commit large amounts of cash in hopes of seeing a larger return. Therefore, make sure the financial commitment matches the overall needs of the group.

To help ensure the group's success, be sure to read about the experiences of other investment groups and make sure all members understand the risks before committing. Also, be careful when forming an investment group with friends. Financial difficulty can strain relationships. Make sure parties have similar goals. You'll want to have a written agreement for the group. A bank or brokerage firm will require articles of incorporation or a partnership agreement when setting up an account. You will also want to record when and how often the group will meet; record an initial membership contribution and ongoing dues; determine how the partnership will manage payouts, divestiture, or dissolution; list requirements for gaining new members once the club has started; and finally, be sure to obtain signatures from all members on the agreement. When started with due diligence, an investment group can not only be a fantastic long-term learning experience, but the profit garnered from it, both financially and socially, will well be worth your investment of time and energy.

Starting an Investment Group

The In-Crowd

To directly participate in high-level real estate projects, some investors turn to real estate investment groups. Though it might sound like this is just a bunch of people getting together to buy real estate, that's not how these groups work. Rather, they're more like small mutual funds that hold one or more large rental properties and allow investors to buy pieces; for example, an investor could buy two apartments in a building. This setup allows you to invest directly in real estate property without any of the headaches that come with being a landlord.

There are a few different types of setups that fall under this heading, but the two main types are basic real estate investment groups and real estate limited partnerships. Each works differently, but the premise is the same: You'd have a direct investment in a larger real estate holding than you could afford on your own.

Not a Club

Many people talk about real estate investment groups when what they're really referring to is investment clubs (discussed later in this chapter). These two vehicles are not the same: Clubs are composed of members who pool funds to buy properties according to group wishes; investors in groups have no vote—other than deciding whether or not to buy in. In virtually all cases, you'd need to make these investments through an advisor, though some groups do offer direct investing. Enter these deals cautiously and only after you've performed due diligence on both the company and the investment property.

Real Estate Groups

Here's the basic layout of a real estate investment group: A company buys (or builds) apartment or office buildings or retail spaces. Then they offer investors the opportunity to buy individual units, effectively enabling them to join the "group." The company manages all aspects of the property, from securing tenants to setting rents to mowing the lawn. The investors pay a percentage of rent receipts to the company in exchange for those services, and pocket the rest.

Buying into Building Blocks

Real estate investment groups let investors buy distinct pieces of a larger investment, rather than a portion of the property as a whole; for example, you'd own one specific apartment rather than 10 percent of a ten-apartment building. Typically, your name would be on the lease as the landlord, but the company would take on all of the associated duties. By participating in more than one group deal, a single investor can hold stakes in multiple large properties. For example, you could buy one apartment in a tower, one office in a building, and one shop in a strip mall, allowing you to diversify into three different types of real estate without having to hold the entire properties.

Vacancy Protection

Most real estate investment group deals offer a form of vacancy protection—something you usually won't have as an individual landlord. Each investor in a property contributes a small percentage of the rent collected from their units into a vacancy pool. Should a unit you own fall vacant, you'd still receive enough cash to cover the mortgage out of the pool until the company secures a new tenant.

Real Estate Investment Clubs

Join the Club

Investing directly in real estate can be daunting when you're first getting started: Buying property is expensive, there's a lot to learn (laws and tax issues, for example), and property maintenance can be overwhelming. Those drawbacks keep a lot of people from participating in real estate investing, despite its many benefits.

. . .

How to Find a Club

To find a real estate investing club near you, visit the National Real Estate Investors Association website (https://nationalreia.org). The site has links to local groups throughout the United States. The association also offers a membership with lots of benefits (like discounts at Home Depot) and free educational resources. Joining an established real estate investment club helps you get up to speed faster, reduces the fear and anxiety that can come from diving into something new without a safety net, and can help you meet your financial goals.

How They're Set Up

Investment clubs (in general) include members who pool their money and make investment decisions as a group. These groups typically have between five and twenty members big enough to pool enough money to invest in real estate and small enough to be manageable. Because there's a lot of money at stake, real estate investment clubs are normally set up as formal business entities with each member listed as a partial owner.

The Structure

Real estate investment clubs are not informal groups. They're usually set up as LLCs (limited liability companies) or partnerships, and each member gets an ownership stake. They have formal by-laws governing the group and the way it invests, including how individual members invest or withdraw money. Normally, they'll elect officers to govern the group.

Most groups require members to commit to a timeframe, agreeing to participate for at least five years (timeframes will vary). A member who decides to leave has to inform the group in writing, as well as find a replacement member that the group approves. Many clubs impose an "early withdrawal" fee on any member who leaves before his or her commitment period is up. When a property is purchased, the group is listed as the buyer and holds the deed. If a mortgage is required, the group is the legal borrower (though members may have to co-sign the loan).

The Money

When the club is formed, the founding members each contribute a lump sum of money. Whether that contribution is a fixed amount or a minimum depends on how the group is set up. It's easier to track when everyone puts in the same amount, but as long as detailed records are kept and all members agree to it, contributions can vary. Latecomers to the club will also have to contribute a lump sum; this usually happens only when a founding member wants to cash out, so he sells his stake to someone new (who has to be approved by the group). Some clubs also require ongoing contributions (smaller than the original lump sum) to be put toward future investments or club (not property) expenses.

Common REI Philosophy

Before joining a real estate investment club, it's important to know your investing philosophy and theirs. For example, if you're interested in apartment buildings for long-term cash flow, don't join a group that's focused on fixing and flipping distressed properties. The club will spell out its investment objectives in the by-laws (or other binding agreement). Solidifying that philosophy helps focus the group and develop an investing strategy.

Pooling Knowledge and Resources

Real estate investment clubs offer some key advantages over going solo. While money is often the first benefit that springs to mind, it's only one way that working with a group can improve your real estate investing experience.

Access to More Properties

Joining a club gives you options that you wouldn't have as a lone real estate investor just starting out. Clubs can have enough funding to buy multiple properties or even commercial real estate (like office buildings), for example.

Knowledge and Skills

Many real estate investing clubs assign roles to members based on their personal background and abilities. Those responsibilities could include:

- Keeping club records
- Bookkeeping and taxes
- Property maintenance
- Tenant management
- Member communications
- Scheduling meetings
- Representing the club at closings
- Researching potential investments

By keeping these jobs "in-house," the club can direct more funds toward building its real estate portfolio or increasing equity.

Splitting the Difference

When only some members take on club-related jobs, the club can decide to give them additional shares of profits, pay them for their services out of club funds, or decrease their original or ongoing investment amount to compensate them for their work.

Education

Investing smarter is the key to long-term prosperity. Club members meet regularly and share any new experiences or knowledge they've gained (for example, if a member had to deal with an eviction). Many investment clubs invite expert speakers to address the group on relevant topics, such as local foreclosure laws or how to analyze different real estate markets. Sometimes, club funds are used to send members to real estate related conferences; the attending members then share what they learned with the whole group.

Networking Connections

Conferences make great networking events. Members can connect with real estate agents, lenders, and other real estate professionals they'd never otherwise come in contact with. Expanding the club's circle of advisors and professionals can offer special access to properties and deals.

Avoid These Issues

Joining a real estate investment club can have distinct disadvantages, so be careful before you commit your time and money to a club that's not the best fit. Like some other types of real estate investments, a club is illiquid, meaning it's very hard to get your money out if you need it. And unlike other investments, this one is personal in nature; you're a member of a group, which means you're personally connected to the other investors (as they are to each other), and that can cause personal problems down the line.

No Flexibility

The biggest drawback to real estate investment clubs is the complete lack of flexibility for members. If you have a sudden need for your money and have to cash out some of your equity, you'd need to get the support of other members, convince another member to buy out your share, or find a new investor that could take your place in the group to buy you out. This process can take months, even longer than the process of selling a property. Plus, if you need your money back before the group's stated minimum time commitment is up, you may have to pay a penalty for leaving (and these can be pretty steep). If you can't afford to tie up this money for at least the commitment period, an investment club may not be the right choice for you.

Emotions Run High

Investment clubs are made up of people and when you combine people and money, emotions are sure to surface. Those feelings can sometimes interfere with sound investment decisions, which can hurt the group's profitability over the long run. For example, some group members can get caught up in the enthusiasm and excitement of a member's property suggestion and overlook property pitfalls. Members may also argue about which properties to buy, hold, or sell. As with any other group of people, clashes can develop between members, cliques can form, and leaders that drive decisions can emerge. Though members try to keep everything strictly professional, it doesn't always work out that way.

Chapter Summary

In this chapter we learnt on Investing in Rental Properties:

- Starting an Investment Group
- Real Estate Groups
- Real Estate Investment Clubs
- How They're Set Up
- Pooling Knowledge and Resources
- Avoiding Issues

In the next chapter you will learn....about how you Invest in Rental Properties

6

INVEST IN RENTAL PROPERTIES

DO you want a vacation home that you aren't paying for? Rental Property investing could be the answer to your second home. Looking ahead to retirement, you can purchase this second home now and rent it out. When you retire, the house will be paid in full and you can decorate it in your own style when you are ready to live full-time. The key you have renters in it paying your mortgage on the home. Of course, the suggestion is painting a "rosy" picture, and there are certain caveats to the situation. Any time you purchase a home with a mortgage, you are going to need a down payment. This down payment can be recouped as part of the rental fee you charge, so in the end you put a little money in, get it back, and have a second home for later in your life.

Rental property investing can be more about a full-time business that is designed to earn you a livable income, for those who are not looking at owning a second home for vacations or retirement. Whatever your goals and objectives are, you will discover how to make your investment work for you. Before you commit to being a real estate investor, you do need to determine if rental property investing is right for you, as well as what is best to buy in terms of your goals. In this book, you learn all about how to determine whether an investment is appropriate, typical investors' goals, what to purchase and how to start a real estate investment strategy.

The procedure will be described in detail, with a focus on the financial aspects, which will make rental property investment attractive and profitable for you. You are also going to be given tips that are designed to help you create a winning strategy and avoid the typical mistakes new investors make. If you follow certain real estate investment plans, then you understand you are likely to make mistakes. Fix and Flip shows like those on HGTV offer some great examples of how not to get into real estate investment, when you don't have the background to do so. First and foremost, you are going to be given a realistic outlook for rental property investing, so you can make an educated, business decision rather than an emotional, hopeful decision as to whether investing is right for you. The individuals who make millions investing in rental properties are able to do so because they treat it like a business and know it takes time and money to accrue their wealth.

Your Objectives and Goals to Invest in Rental Property?

Part of figuring out whether or not rental property investing is right for you is to understand your goals and objectives. What do you hope to gain from rental property investments that might alleviate certain risks and bring more rewards? Let's explore some of the most popular objectives people have for starting a rental property investing business.

Full Income Replacement

It is possible to gain full income from renting properties. However, it is not going to happen overnight. It will take an investment strategy that minimizes the risks and provides higher rewards. To gain full income, you will need to invest your money with the idea of lowering your risks. For full income replacement, you will need more than one property. You could go in with the idea of purchasing one property with the money you have, ensuring the property is completely paid for, but then you would not have money to purchase two or three more properties.

While at the beginning, you would have multiple mortgages to pay, you will also have the rent to pay those mortgages. The rent will be designed to provide enough cash flow to pay the mortgage, plus provide you with full income to replace a 9 to 5 job at a desk. Your job will become one that researches various properties to purchase, rent, and earn the income from the rents paid.

Supplement Regular Income

If you are not ready to give up on your current job, but wish to have more income, then you may decide to use rental property investing to supplement your regular income. For example, you may have one or two rental properties that not only have cover for the mortgage on them, but provide you with a little savings or extra money to spend. In this situation you will have a part time job.

Multi-Family Unit for Rent Free Living

Do you want to own your home, without being responsible for the mortgage? Duplexes or other multi-family homes can be the answer. If you own a duplex, then you can live on one side, while another renter lives on the other side. In this situation, you would have the rent set high enough to cover the mortgage and provide a secondary source of income. Your renter basically pays for you to own the house. You can also do this with mother-in-law apartments attached to regular homes. If you have a basement or space on your lot to add to your home, you could create an entire apartment to rent out and have the money from that rent cover your mortgage.

Solid Source of Retirement Income

For some, there is an objective of gaining rental properties for the purpose of making retirement savings. It is a possibility. This objective works two ways. First, you have the rent set at a level that will cover the mortgage on the property and provide you with supplemental income. Second, you gain equity as the mortgage decreases and the home value increases. When you are ready to retire, you can sell the home for the increased value and take that money for retirement costs.

Purchasing a Vacation Home

Rental property investing can also have an objective of helping you purchase a vacation property. You will need to decide how you wish to go about this, but it can work in two ways. You purchase a property, with a mortgage and rent it out full time. The rental fee for the property goes to paying the mortgage and provides you with extra income. The other option is to use it as a vacation rental property. If it is a vacation rental property, then you have a few weeks, perhaps a couple of months with various tenants coming and going, but you also get to use the home.

For this second option to work, you will need to block out certain times in the year that you wish to use your home. At all other times, you have various renters coming and going. With this concept, you can charge a little more per "night" than you would for a regular rental. For example, some people charge $150 per night, with a minimum four-day stay.

During this period, one can make $600. Depending on the mortgage just one renter for $600 a month may be enough to cover the expense and all other renters are extra income for you.

The upside is that you are purchasing a vacation home to use full time, once the mortgage is paid off. The downside is you will need to advertise for a rental property and make enough to cover the mortgage during the height of the tourist season or throughout the year.

How Right Is Rental Property Investing?

Any financial decision you make should be made based on the advantages and disadvantages, with a business outlook. Hearing other people's investment stories can get you excited. You can begin to believe you too can make millions investing, but the reality is each person has a different situation, different goals, and it is better to assess whether rental property investing is right for you based on the benefits and risks.

. . .

Benefits

From a business perspective, there are five benefits for you to consider:

- Tangible asset
- Current income
- Appreciation
- Leverage
- Tax advantages

Tangible Asset

When you invest in property, you have a tangible asset, something that you can see and touch, which is different from most investment strategies. When you own shares of a company, you don't actually set foot in the company, but reap the benefits of that investment. With rental property, you are going to own the building and the land, or at least a portion of it.

Current Income

Current income is what you make after you have paid the mortgage and other related expenses. Depending on whether you pay for the energy, water, sewer, trash, or not, you will need to determine how much you will make in income after all those expenses are paid. Most individuals who run rental properties will have mortgages when they first start out, so the rent is based on what the mortgage will be plus other expenses, including maintenance costs, and a determination of how much you can add on top of that total.

For example, if you are charging $1100 for a rental property, and you want $400 in profit, then your mortgage, rental property insurance, and other expenses cannot be more than $700 per month. On the other hand, if the mortgage is already $1100, then you would not be charging enough to make an income and would be in a deficit. Later on, you'll learn how to figure rental property fees for profit.

· · ·

Appreciation or Equity

Appreciation is a term assigned to an increase in value for something. If the value increases, then it appreciates; however, if the value decreases it will depreciate. Appreciation is something you want to see with your property. You want it to increase in value, so you have more equity in the home. Equity is the difference of value minus the mortgage owed. It is what you can pull out as cash when you do an equity mortgage or what you would earn if you sold the property for its full value and paid off the current mortgage amount.

A house does not have to appreciate value. It can depreciate depending on the current market. For example, the subprime mortgage crisis occurred for two reasons. One, banks provided loans to people who couldn't really afford them. Two, many houses were overvalued, so the housing boom imploded. Houses started depreciating to the point that when they were sold they couldn't cover the mortgage costs, let alone return a profit.

Appreciation would be nice if it occurred all the time and could be in the benefit column at all times. However, you have to realize that certain properties, mainly in cities, are already overvalued and less likely to appreciate. If a home appreciates, it is a benefit to you.

Leverage

Leverage is what you can borrow. It goes back to the equity in a home. If you have accrued equity because of housing appreciation, then you have a potential of getting a second loan on one rental property and buying another property with that money. By using the equity, you are using an asset to secure the loan, but you are not using your main home for the new property, making your situation slightly more secure. If something happens and you cannot repay the loans, then you lose the secondary properties versus your main home.

Tax Advantages

There is a possibility of owning a second home without incurring more federal taxes. If your property is not providing a net cash flow once expenses are deducted, then you do not have to pay taxes. You are gaining income, but because the expenses are either creating a deficit or causing you to break even, you don't have to pay taxes. It is also possible to refinance the loan on the property when it appreciates and take advantage of falling interest rates, without tax issues. There are also certain situations, where you can sell a rental property and reinvest the money, without incurring taxes on the sale of the home. These tax advantages are something you would need to discuss with your accountant.

The main focus for tax advantages should be the reinvestment of your funds, as a means of avoiding paying taxes versus being in a negative income situation with the property. The idea of investing is to gain a profit and income to spend, but you also have to be aware of the taxes that can come with this.

What Property Is Right to Investment In?

Creating an investment strategy should be about what you are most comfortable with, not only in terms of risk, but what you know. People make the mistake of starting off a new project expecting everything to be easy once they read a book. However, rental property investing should not be taken lightly. There are risks. If you have never owned an apartment complex, let alone understand the maintenance and costs that go with owning such a place, you will want to build up to it or be a partner. Partnering in an investment where a management company takes care of the day to day running of things may suit you better. To help you determine what property you should invest in, we will explore the different investment options.

Condos

Condos can be purchased and rented out in certain locations. Many tourist towns allow condos to be purchased for the purpose of vacation rentals. You will need to check with the HOA to make certain there are no restrictions.

Benefits

- You can own a condo in your same building or area, if you already own a condo.
- Outside maintenance for condo buildings is taken care of by the HOA.
- It is a single unit, within a community and may be used as vacation or full time rental.

Disadvantages

- Some HOAs prohibit the rental of owned condos.
- There are HOA requirements for what you can do to the exterior of the building, such as installing internet, satellites, or changing the color of your condo.
- You are responsible for your backyard or front yard area, while the HOA is taking care of the exterior building and any community lawn areas.
- There are neighbors and you may be restricted on what you can do regarding the rental.

Commercial Property

Commercial property certainly offers a different rental property investment, then the others previously discussed. With commercial property, you are looking for businesses. In recent years, brick and mortar businesses have suffered due to online purchases. Commercial property can also require a larger investment. However, there are definitely advantages and disadvantages to this option that may suit your investment goals.

Benefits

- Businesses tend to pay more in rent, thus it may be easier for you to switch to rental property investing as a full time income.
- You can have multiple units in the same building, thus gain more tenants.

Disadvantages

- You will need a commercial property liability insurance policy, which is expensive.
- The initial investment will be larger.
- You may need partners, who will also need to make decisions.
- Maintenance of commercial property is higher.
- You may find it difficult to keep tenants if you choose the wrong area or you may only have one tenant versus a fully rented building.

Overall, your expenses and the initial investment are more, but so is the reward.

As you can see, you have multiple options when it comes to the types of properties you can invest in. It is up to you how you will structure your rental investment strategy, but it should fit within your knowledge base and investment abilities. You do not want to overextend yourself due to the high risks involved.

Identify What to Buy

Now that you have an explanation of options, it is time to consider what would be best to purchase for your investment needs. This will go back to what your goals are.

- How much income do you want from your real estate investment?

- Do you know anything about maintaining apartment complexes or commercial property?
- Do you know the real estate laws for the different properties or is your knowledge better suited to a single family or duplex dwelling?

Identifying what to buy is not only about what is available on the market, but whether one property fits into your real estate investment objectives and goals better than another.

Single Family Residence

Often this is the best choice for beginners. You already own a home or have purchased a home recently, so you have an idea of the running costs and maintenance you will need for a rental property. You might have decided to rent out the home you currently live in as a way to move into a larger single-family residence. As standalone units, you know that you are responsible for all the maintenance. You also need to have energy, water, and sewer hooked up based on the house address versus trying to determine what multiple residents would require. For many people the single-family residence is easiest because it can be used for a vacation rental or a second home in a place you enjoy travelling.

Benefits

- You will have one renter or a family versus multiple people to keep track of.
- You can choose the home based on popular size. Each market is different throughout the nation, but you want to have a home that is going to rent, which often comes down to size, bathrooms, and bedrooms.
- The renter can set up their own utilities, so you are not responsible for the payments each month or how much usage. It saves you from having to lose money in the event your

renters use more utilities than you allotted for in the rent payment.
- It is also one structure to maintain versus many.

Disadvantages

- You are responsible for the lawn work and outside upkeep, versus a condo where you'd have an HOA.
- You have only one rental income and would need multiple homes to rent to make single family units a way to make a full income.
- If you need a mortgage for the property, there is only one renter responsible. If there is a vacancy for a while, you would be paying the mortgage without help.

Duplex/Triplex/Quad

Multi-family dwellings such as duplexes can make a great deal of sense. You can live in one unit, while you have renters on the other side. In this setup, you would have someone paying rent that would cover the mortgage you have on the place. With more than two units, you can also afford one being vacant for a short time and feel confident that you have the mortgage payment. Multi-unit homes are great for college and university towns. They can also be great in areas where housing is difficult to find or in areas of lower rent requirements. Of course, each option will have benefits and disadvantages.

Benefits

- Someone helps pay the rent.
- You have multiple units to rent at the same time.
- You still have one building to maintain.

Disadvantages

- You may need to share a wall with renters, if you are going to live in the same structure.
- You will either need multiple utility meters or devise a utility payment that is fair, without you being at a disadvantage.
- You have more units to rent.

Apartment Buildings

It is rare for a person to have enough of an investment to own an apartment building outright. Typically, individuals who are thinking about rental property investment, are individuals looking to fulfill a goal to increase their income versus already having millions to invest. If you intend on investing in apartment buildings, you are going to need to find a management group that offers you the best situation. There are certain benefits to owning an apartment building, even in part. You may also find a small dwelling with four or more apartments that you could afford without investors. It will take research to find the correct location for your rental property investment goals.

Benefits

- As a part of a management group with other investors the risk is lower.
- The investment can work where you have a specific unit assigned to you or not. However, if a unit stands empty, then everyone still makes a profit if the location is making a profit because the rental income is shared.
- You also have a company set up to take the liability versus the personal liability you can sustain as an individual landowner.

Disadvantages

- Rental interest can change, where you can be too full or too empty. If multiple units are empty you may not make a profit.
- You are a part of a group, so group decisions will need to be made.

- If your unit is not empty, but another is, you still have to cover the mortgage and then share any profit.
- Apartment buildings require more maintenance.
- Utilities are harder to assign because it is based on the number of units, not necessarily what people use. You may find some months your expenses are more than in other months.

Risks of Rental Property Investments

With benefits, come downsides. Owning rental property is not for everyone because of the risks you may face.

Here are the top disadvantages:

- Liability
- Unexpected expenses
- Bad tenants
- Vacancy
- Eviction expenses
- Insurance issues
- Advertising fees
- Attorney fees

Liability

Liability can lead to unexpected expenses, insurance claims, and more money out of your pocket. If a tenant falls on your property they can sue you for "emotional distress." While both you and the tenant share responsibility, you are required to ensure your rental property is up to government codes. If there is even a little something wrong, you could end up paying for it.

Unexpected Expenses

Unexpected expenses can come from a variety of situations, such as a water heater that is 30 years old that suddenly breaks. Repairs to the home may also be something that you will have to cover. For example, a bad tenant might leave your rental property in disrepair to the point that even their deposit doesn't cover the damage. Faulty wiring, foundation issues, roof repair or replacement, and a host of other things can go wrong with a property depending on its age and build quality.

Bad Tenants

Not only can bad tenants leave you with a destroyed property, but they can leave you with months of rent owed. You may need to have a collection agency get the rent or worse, you may never be able to see that money. In some instances, tenants will turn around and try to sue you.

Eviction Expenses

Eviction expenses come along with bad tenants. If you have to file eviction documents with the court and have cops come out to remove the individuals from your premises, you will have to foot that bill. Even if the court sides in your favor, you may still not receive the rent owed or any money for damages sustained during the eviction process.

Vacancy

Bad tenants are to be feared, just as much as having a rental property vacant. A vacant rental property means you are covering the mortgage you have on the property, as well as any other expenses like energy costs.

Insurance Issues

Issues such as insurance liability claims are just the beginning. You may also encounter homeowner insurance issues; such as being covered for certain things that can happen when you rent a place. Furthermore, any insurance claim filed for repairs on a home can take weeks, sometimes months to pay out. Insurance for a rental space can also be extremely costly, since you have to cover damage that a tenant might do like causing a fire.

Advertising Fees

A part of ensuring your rental property gets rented, is advertising that you have a place for rent. Advertising fees can be exorbitant depending on where you place your ads. Online sites like Craigslist may lead you to a proper tenant, but a lot of trouble has arisen from these free sites. If you are not paying for advertising, then you are still paying an agency to run background checks on your tenants for your peace of mind.

Attorney Fees

Attorney fees may need to be paid for several reasons, such as drafting tenant documents and filing for the eviction process. These fees can decrease your income or even wipe out what income you were making on renting a property.

As you can see, there is a long list of risks involved in rental property investing. These risks are some of the reasons many investors decide to buy into a group management rental property, such as an apartment complex that they share ownership with. The risks become slightly less, when there are other people involved to hold some of the responsibility.

You should know that nearly every person that has tried or even succeeded in rental property investing has at least one bad tenant story. You have to decide if you are willing to take on at least one very risky situation in order to reap the rewards that will come from rental property investing.

Think about this checklist:

- Do you have the income to support two mortgages?
- Are you willing to lose a property if you default on the mortgage and take the credit score hit that comes along with it?
- Do you have the time to be a landlord, checking on the home and maintaining it?
- When you calculate the type of rental property investing, you wish to do based on expenses and potential income, is there enough income to make it worth it?

With this last bullet point, you will need to do a lot of research before you can determine if you are willing to take on the responsibilities and risks of renting property in order to gain the benefits. Given the various types of rental property investment, you may find something that suits your risk/reward ratio enough to still invest.

Things to Consider

They are easier to resell

You may not want to own a particular piece of the property forever. A single-family unit can appeal to a broader market for resale than a multi-family unit would. Since it appeals to both owner-occupiers and investors, they can be easier to sell.

They have lower operating costs

Usually, tenants in a single-family dwelling will pay for all of their utilities. It will result in considerable savings to you, the owner. And even if you own several single-family units, their costs for expenses are usually lower since not all companies will need a new roof or new floors at the same time.

You have greater flexibility over your portfolio growth

If you purchase a multifamily unit, you have to buy the entire building at once. It can be a substantial monetary investment. But in purchasing single-family units, you can buy them one at a time and watch your portfolio grow larger over time. You will also have the flexibility to sell off units that may no longer be profitable.

Average local rents

Since you will be making your money from the rental income, you will need to know the area's average rent. And whatever you decide to charge for rent will need to cover your expenses for the property, taxes, insurance, and mortgage payment.

Natural disasters

Since the homeowner's insurance is one of the expenses the rent will need to cover, you will need to know upfront how much insurance you will need and what it will cost. Houses located in areas that flood or have earthquakes might not support the rent required to cover the extra insurance.

Local vacancies and listings

If there are several listings or vacancies, it might be a seasonal thing, meaning the area is declining. Most of the tenants move during summer months to settle before the subsequent school year; many listings in June are not as bothersome as the same quantity of listings in October. An area with a high vacancy rate will not support the rent you might need to make positive cash flow.

Possible future development

Any new growth and development in the area will be the local planning and development office's responsibility, so check with them before purchasing a rental dwelling. Future rezoning could help or hurt your investment. Future planned development of a shopping center nearby will benefit your investment. The result of a recycling center would probably hurt your chances of renting your investment to a tenant.

Local amenities

Drive around the neighborhood and look for public libraries, parks, public transportation, movie theaters, gyms, and restaurants. These are amenities that people like to have near either where they work or where they live.

Local habits

Also, take a drive through the neighborhood on different days and at other times of the day and night. A quiet and peaceful setting on Sunday afternoon might turn into a block party on Saturday night.

Your new tenant might not like that, so you need to know these things upfront before buying.

Local job market

Tenants will be more attracted to areas that have job availability if needed. The local government can give you statistics on job availability for a particular location. Check and see if new businesses are opening up in the areas because new companies require new employees, and those employees need somewhere to live.

Crime rates

Check the frequency of criminal activity in the area where you plan to buy a rental property. Look at the rates for petty crimes and serious crimes and the rates for burglary and vandalism. No one wants to move into a high crime area, and that perfect rental property might be less than ideal if it is in an area prone to crime.

Schools

Purchasing a home sufficient enough for a family will mean that the area needs to support good schools. Accepting a house in a place where there are substandard schools or no schools will seriously affect your ability to rent and affect its resale value in the future.

Assessed property taxes

The property's location will have a significant effect on the amount of property tax you will be required to pay. The tariffs will need to be paid out of the money you are paid for the monthly rent. A great neighborhood with classier homes will support the higher property taxes required, but plenty of downtrodden communities have high property taxes. It is also good to verify the town's financial stability because future property tax hikes used to cover government costs can price you right out of the market.

Neighborhood

It is probably the most crucial consideration. The neighborhood will be a determining factor in lowering your vacancy rates and attracting good tenants. It might be easy to find tenants for a house near a college in August, but will the house still be occupied the following July? A neighborhood near a highway might be attractive to renters who commute downtown for work every day but not appealing to a young couple with children.

Chapter Summary

In this chapter we learnt on Joining a Real Estate Investment Group:

- Setting Your Objectives and Goals to Invest in Rental Property
- How Right Is Rental Property Investing
- What Property Is Right to Investment In
- Risks of Rental Property Investments
- Things to Consider

In the next chapter you will learn....about Tip For Veterans & Active-Duty Service Members

7

BONUS TIP - FOR VETERANS & ACTIVE-DUTY SERVICE MEMBERS

REAL ESTATE: everyone is talking about it. It looks like we all know someone who knows someone who has become very successful thanks to it. Unfortunately, because of how profitable it can be, people often classify it as one of those businesses for rich people rather than what it actually is: One of those businesses that make people rich. If you have decided to venture into the world of real estate, have a seat. Before you can effectively make anything out of this world, you have to understand it completely. Real estate does not favor impulsive businessmen or people who do not have sufficient knowledge. Before doing anything, you must study.

Possessing a house is a long-standing benchmark for having accomplished the American Dream. It is just normal for American veterans to need to take an interest in this central part of living in the U.S.. Subsequent to working for their country, veterans are likely looking for the security and roots that house purchasing offers—contrasted with leasing. Home purchasing is usually distressing, even the individuals who have effectively bought a property. Since veterans spend a lot of their time traveling, it might add to the pressure that can go with the cycle. It might assist exploring a few hints and assets with regards to investing resources into a property. From settling on a geographic area, deciding monetary stuff and knowing the local housing market, veterans may require some help.

Types of Financial Options Accessible by Veterans

Monetary counselors and realtors know it is essential to help veterans acquire the correct property. With regards to financing the acquisition of that property, they may require the support of a fair monetary consultant to address questions and facilitate the cycle. Monetary counselors comprehend that veterans are a pivotal factor in home purchasing socioeconomics and endeavor to make the interaction simpler. Monetary experts assist veterans with exploring issues which include recognizing and avoiding ruthless loaning schemes and dealing with the monetary issues that frequently go with the change from military to regular citizen life.

Ideally, veterans begin putting something aside for their dream house when they join the military. One regular suggestion from monetary counsels is that the military work force start an in-depth saving plan at the earliest in their military profession. Deployment isn't a snag since the Department of Defense offers a unique Savings Deposit Program. With this, military staff can contribute up to $10,000 for a 10% return once abroad for 30 days. Impressively, they can collect their interest for an extra 120 days after returning back to the U.S. When veterans start to explore the monetary chances accessible to them, they will discover sensible monetary arrangements that fit their conditions.

VA Loan Eligibility Requirements

To be qualified for a VA advance, you or your life partner should meet the fundamental help prerequisites set by the Department of Veterans Affairs (VA), have a legitimate Certificate of Eligibility (COE) and fulfill the bank's credit and pay necessities.

You may be eligible for a VA loan by meeting one or more of the following requirements:

- You have worked 181 days of active service during peacetime, OR
- You have served 90 consecutive days of active service during wartime, OR
- You are the spouse of a service member who has died in the line of duty or as a result of a service-related disability.
- You have 6 years of service in the National Guard or Reserves

Best Real Estate Advices for Veterans Wanting to Invest

Once veterans decide that they need to buy a home, it is nice to begin looking for approaches to save and invest. There are a lot of things everybody can do to get ready for this undertaking

- **Start Saving.** It is never too soon to begin saving for future use. When veterans or dynamic military faculty begin planning

ahead, particularly with regards to purchasing a home, it is a nice chance to begin savings.
- **Explore VA Loans for the Lowest Rates.** VA center home buying loans alongside a few other loans for exceptional conditions.
- **Track Credit Score.** Ordinarily, loans require a specific financial assessment. It is significant that veterans keep a sound financial assessment to make a point to try not to pass up loans opportunities. Active military staff can get a Bright-Score report free of charge, which incorporates a credit report and tips on improving that score.
- **Pay Down Debt.** For anybody with any debt, it assists with paying that down straightaway to raise one's FICO rating and lower the home loan rate. It may assist with taking care of credit cards and credit, look for low or no deposit loans for veterans.
- **Search for a Good Real Estate Agent.** It is essential to have great individuals helping you to buy your home. Working with a good real estate agent will help lessen the leg work and build assurance in the procedure. These experts likewise help discover extra answers for veterans
- **Consider Take-Home Pay.** Investigate what it is possible to easily pay. Veterans should restrict the expense of housing including insurance, duties, upkeep and utilities to 30% of salary.

Luckily, there is additionally a lot of monetary help accessible for veterans. Ex-military staff should exploit assets explicitly assigned for them like VA-supported loans for unexpected projects, states and locality programs. Taking on the home purchasing process is tedious and disappointing, however by fostering a solid methodology and exploiting the accessible assets makes it a lot simpler.

Real Estate Investing While in Active Service for U.S. Military

This guide is intended to fill in as a beginning spot for those hoping to invest into real estate whereas serving in the U.S. military. I 100% served in our military, so I'm composing this from the viewpoint of somebody who has a very decent comprehension of the U.S. investing world and appreciates clarifying things! Clearly, there are sections of the military, has a range of occupations, obligations, duties, pay scales, and areas for those serving.

You may be situated inside the U.S., or you might be serving outside. You might have a family, or you might be staying alone. Possibly you are full time, or maybe you are a "end of the week hero." Possibly you've been in the military for quite a long time and make an extraordinary compensation, or perhaps you are recently out of training camp. Each investing technique ought to be planned around where your capabilities, finances, and objectives meet. The best focal point of this guide will be on investing resources into real estate when your area isn't guaranteed to be the same always, as this is by all accounts the best obstacle for those hoping to invest into real estate whereas serving under the U.S. military. In spite of the fact that it is important to know the region you invest in, it isn't needed. What's more, this guide will show you various techniques you can use to keep your location and your investing methodology discrete.

Why Invest in Real Estate While Serving in the Military?

For every one of the incredible things that can be said about Uncle Sam, few would utilize "liberal with remuneration" to depict our government. I doubt a lot of that you enrolled into the military to become rich (all things considered, there is an explanation it is called "serving in the military.") Notwithstanding, you presumably have dreams, expectations, and desires for your future and family which will need more pay than you'll probably make from your profession. While usual individual finance guidance is to just "save more," it's insufficient to just set aside cash except if that set aside cash has a higher reason. All in all, you can't build wealth 'till your cash is functioning to make you more money.

Choosing Real Estate over Other Investing Strategies

Of the multitude of ventures to invest in out there, I immovably admit the best is land. I agree no other venture on earth gives a similar potential for building enduring abundance than land investing. For beginners, real estate investing provides:

- The capacity to utilize influence to boost your outcomes (applying a little initial installment to control an immense resource)
- Past stability and development
- Various approaches to produce abundance (month to month cash from the rental pay, appreciation when costs go up, tax cuts, and then some)

The capacity for you to straightforwardly affect the aftereffects of your speculation (dissimilar to other latent ventures like shared assets where your monetary predetermination lies in the possession of obscure workers on Wall Street)

In any case, real estate isn't equivalent to other different ventures. It requires a specific arrangement of abilities and obligation to accomplish the mind boggling results you are searching for. Investing resources into real estate for incredible returns takes planning, tolerance, and information. It takes hard work. I know the final product merits the exertion in view of the capability of more noteworthy benefits. Notwithstanding, the basic inquiry exists: Are 12% consistent returns possible? Therefore is investing in real estate a good idea for active service members of the military? Yes.

The remainder of this guide will show you various techniques you can use to accomplish unfathomable outcomes while keeping your investments sufficiently autonomous from your ventures so that you can keep on serving your country in the military.

Job vs. Investment

A typical issue among those hoping to begin investing in real estate includes the disarray between investing resources into real estate being a job and investing resources into real estate being an investment. It gets significantly more befuddling in light of the fact that the two are not in every case effectively discernible even to those that are involved each day in this industry.

Maybe you've seen the TV shows where investors purchase a modest house, fix it up, and sell it, expecting to make enormous benefits? That is called "house flipping" is a popular and theoretically lucrative job however is normally considered to be a "job." Once the "flipper" ends flipping, the cash stops too. An investment, however, continues to yield income after you stop inputting your cash producing.

There isn't anything amiss with real estate as a "job," however I need to urge you to keep the two separate. You don't have to dedicate 40 hours per week to real estate as an investment. All things considered, you are a military officer; you most likely don't have the opportunity! By zeroing in on the "venture" part, you could make abundance and automated revenue for your future. The remainder of this guide will zero in on "investment" of real estate, explicitly purchasing and leasing single-family or multifamily properties.

How Would You Invest Whereas in the Military?

As previously mentioned, there are several means to invest into real estate. It is, thus, important to recognize a few diverse strategies hence you could best decide which fits into your lifestyle. Below are a number of the very common approaches utilized by those serving in the military.

Owner-Occupant Investing

Perhaps the coolest advantage for dynamic and ex- U.S. Military individuals, the VA credit is a funding (it's in fact advance insurance for the bank, however that is not essential for now) given by the government to assist you with acquiring a home loan with no cash down. Yes, zero % down payment. You could even make the seller to recompense a lot of the concluding costs, for you to get into the property with nearly nothing from your pocket.

In any case, what does purchasing an occupied house have on investing? Nevertheless, a house is not actually a plentiful investment. (Not logically thinking. Sure, the price can increase, but that is only a notion.) Conversely, there are 2 common circumstances that can make a property holder to an investor:

Home to Rental: Numerous U.S. Military active members end up relocating—a lot. For different reasons, you may end up with your family being posted to countless bases in the U.S military if you aren't serving overseas. Subsequently, several military families turn to real estate investors by accident, by essentially transforming their current home into a rental every time they are moved.

Small Multifamily: A multifamily property could be a triplex, duplex, or fourplex. Furthermore, several loans, including the VA loan, believe these properties as equivalent to a solitary family house. At the end of the day, you could live on one unit while leasing the other unit(s) to cater for the home loan installment or more. Both these techniques can be utilized by individuals from the military (or anybody,) to begin investing away with basically no cash down.

Turnkey

Perhaps the most common mainstream alternatives for investing resources into real estate while keeping up the area autonomy is by "turnkey" real estate. Despite the fact that there are contrasts in how each organization works, they all exist to give an "all in one shop" for purchasing and renting real estate. As such, they can locate assets for you, assist you with acquiring financing, deal with the occupants, and deal with a large portion of the accounting. Sounds too good to be real?

There is a great deal of discussion on the viability of turnkey real estate, which is generally founded on singular encounters with certain turnkey suppliers. Clearly, the turnkey organization needs to make a benefit, so you may pay a higher premium for the property than you may somehow pay all alone. Then again, turnkey organizations will in general bargain for more ideal arrangements since they are prepared to comprehend their market, and their plan of action is attached to rehashing clients and effective ventures for their customers.

Partner Up

On the chance that you need to begin investing yet don't have the opportunity or information to do so the other techniques laid out in this guide you might consider collaborating with an accomplished investor who can aid you set up your cash to work. As an individual from the armed services, you have a significant attribute: You are in employment. All in all, you most likely can get housing contracts besides you might even have some money set aside. While you may come up short on the area setting up an agreement, there might be another investor out there with an area yet does not have the money, credit, or occupation history. Good partnering unites numerous parties with various qualities to achieve objectives that they couldn't do alone. Check at which traits you possess. What could you provide to the deal? It's not difficult to rapidly filter through the individuals who appear to understand what they are discussing versus the individuals who don't. Begin building associations with various Bigger Pockets individuals today. No one can tell where those connections may lead.

Crowdfunding

This is one of the modern spectacles in real estate investing today. Crowdfunding; it is the procedure of conveying together several investors into an investment in real estate all together. Numerous portals, like Fundrise or RealtyMogul, have extended traction as money making, yet passive, approaches for capitalizing in real estate minus necessitating getting your hands tedious. Crowdfunding being relatively new to the real estate investment world, the guidelines are quite a little fuzzy about where the business is heading (and what precisely is lawful to do). Nonetheless society does appear to be accepting progressively more crowdfunded real estate investment deals.

Chapter Summary

In this chapter we learnt on Tips—For Veterans & Active-Duty Service Members:

- Types of Financial Options Accessible by Veterans
- Best Real Estate Advices for Veterans Wanting to Invest
- Real Estate Investing While in Active Service for U.S. Military
- Why Invest in Real Estate While Serving in the Military?
- Choosing Real Estate over Other Investing Strategies
- How Would You Invest Whereas in the Military

In the next chapter you will learn....about Real-Estate Moguls Success Stories

8

REAL-ESTATE MOGULS - THE SUCCESS STORIES

Learning from Others

ONCE YOU DO START GETTING into the how-to guides for various real estate investment strategies, you might notice a lot of them only tell you how to do the strategy while not necessarily painting the whole picture of the strategy. Few how-to guides offer a rating system for the effort level, skill level, and frustration level that come with each of the strategies. One of the best ways to better understand different real estate investing strategies is to hear about them directly from experienced investors who are already succeeding with them.

- What's the actual reality I can expect with this strategy?
- Is the strategy overly difficult?
- What skills will I really need?
- What are the risks with the strategy?
- How can I help mitigate those risks?
- Will I like this strategy?

As I said numerous times throughout the book, your investing isn't going to look 100% like someone else's investing (which is why the how-to guides by themselves don't usually work). The key really is in gathering as much information as you can about the different strategies, self-assessing where your skills, strengths, and interests are, and coming up with a plan based on those. To help in gathering all of that information, I interviewed successful real estate investors who all do different strategies. The intention with these interviews is to help give you that real-life perspective on what some of these strategies look like once you really get into them. You still aren't going to have all the answers once you go through these, but you will have more information to help you assess what path you may want to think about pursuing.

While you never want to take advantage of the opportunity to connect with successful investors by demanding them help you or asking them to teach you everything they know for free, it can be very valuable to connect with people who have already paved their own path and can share their experiences. This is why I purposefully selected the investors that I did for these interviews. All of them currently mentor individuals in their selected strategies. Many of them have created their own training programs, some of them lead local real estate meetups, and most of them offer a lot of valuable resources online. At the end of each interview will be the investor's bio and links to be able to connect with them. Reach out to them if their strategy seems to resonate with you!

Sharon Vornholt

Location of investments: Louisville, KY, 21 years' experience, 11 years wholesaling

Q: Can you describe your investment strategy?

A: I am a wholesaler at this time, however I have also been a rehabber and a buy-and-hold landlord. I was a rehabber and a buy and hold landlord for 10 years until the crash in 1998. That's when I became an "accidental wholesaler".

I specialize in probates, as well as marketing and branding your real estate business. Probate is a legal process of administering a deceased person's estate. This includes establishing their money, possessions and assets and allocating them as estate, after paying out any debts and taxes. Investors provide a valuable service to these folks since they have to sell the property in the estate

Real property like houses, land, etc. must be sold to pay the creditors, before the heirs can get what they are inheriting. The creditors include anyone that is owed money like outstanding loans or mortgages, credit cards, hospital and nursing home bills, and funeral expenses.

Many times, the property in the estate is a distressed property that would need a lot of work before it could be listed on the MLS and the heirs don't want to spend their time or money doing this. Since the property **must** be sold to settle the estate (unless it was directly inherited or part of a trust), these folks can be very motivated sellers. As a wholesaler, this is very advantageous for me in terms of where I find the properties that I wholesale.

Q: How much time do you typically spend on your investments?

A: It used to be my full-time job. I spend 25-35 hours a week currently. Today I have someone that takes care of that side of the business, so I can focus on the education side of my business. I teach investors marketing, branding and how to build a profitable probate investing business.

No two days are alike for me!

Q: Can you walk us through a typical deal?

A: The timeline: 2 weeks or less in most cases. Probates may take a little longer to close, but the process is the same.

1. *Find a deal through the marketing strategies you are using in your business.* Have 3-5 marketing channels to find deals. Take the

seller calls you get from your marketing. Look at the properties you're interested in. (note: I have to know how to analyze properties so I can know which properties I'm interested in.)
2. *Make the offer to the seller. Negotiate if necessary.*
3. *Write up the contract to buy the property.*
4. *Call my buyer's list and sell the property to one of them.* Call the buyer on my list I think will want this particular property (I know my buyers).
5. *Write the contract to sell the property.*
6. *Send both contracts to my closing attorney.*
7. *Go to closing and do a double-close using none of my own money.*
8. *Pick up a big check.*

Q: What skills do you use regularly for your strategy?

A: *#1 – Marketing*

Marketing is a real estate investor's number one job. If you don't have a steady stream of leads coming in the door you will be out of business in no time.

Think of it this way; if you don't have leads coming in the door you really don't need to know any of the rest of the things like building rapport with sellers, negotiation etc. When it comes to probate investing, marketing to those folks is a different skill set. Your brand (which showcases your expertise) is critical to getting these sellers to choose you. They have to see you as the expert.

#2 – Branding

As I said, having a strong brand makes all your marketing work better because it showcases your expertise and presents you as the expert.

"Marketing is how you get leads. Branding is why they choose YOU".

When it comes to branding, your brand is how you make people feel.

It's also the know, like and trust factor that you are creating with your brand. Branding is what supercharges all your marketing. Some people think branding is just colors, fonts and logos and those are certainly part of the physical aspects of your brand. However, as I said, your brand is how you make people feel. It's also what they say about you when you leave the room; whether you are trustworthy, easy to work with, whether you are the person that brings them great deals.

When it comes to branding here are some things you must do:

- You must have a website. People judge whether you are a "real business" by whether you have a professional looking website.
- You need to build a strong social media presence. This is the perfect place for people to learn about what you do.
- Creating some type of content will build trust and credibility for you and your business. Video is one of the quickest ways to build your brand whether that is through Facebook lives, or videos that you make and post on your website and social media. They don't have to be fancy. People are looking for authenticity.
- Become a networking ninja. You want people to think of you when they have a deal to sell. The only way for that to happen is for you to get out and meet people. Attend your local REIA meeting and volunteer.

#3 – People skills/building rapport (problem solving)

This is a must. You have to be able to talk to sellers in a way that helps solve their problem to be successful as a real estate investor. We are really in the problem-solving business.

If you have a truly motivated seller, they have a problem or an immediate need. They may have a house in probate that they must sell in order to settle the estate. Or, they may have a situation where there is an immediate need or a financial reason, they become a motivated seller. Maybe they have lost their job; they have to relocate quickly to another state; maybe they are getting a divorce or there is some other reason. Whatever that reason is, they have a problem. They have a house they must sell quickly. You are there to help solve their problem, but you always want to create a "win-win" situation for everyone involved.

I would like to point out that these are not always distressed properties. People are often willing to give up some equity for a quick sale that solves their underlying problem like a job transfer or probate property.

However, when it comes to distressed property, the numbers are the numbers. You can only offer what the property is worth no matter what their situation is. You might be able to offer them a creative solution where they get more money for the property, but you get better terms. Great deals are created not found.

#4 – *Negotiating*

I am always negotiating directly with the seller or the executor of the estate if it's a probate since I only work off market deals. On a rare occasion I might work with an agent if it's a pocket deal.

Negotiation is always about the price and/or the terms. One way of negotiating is to go for a low, cash offer to the seller. You might also do deals where the terms of the deal are more important than the price. For example, you might pay more for a property if the sellers will do a low or no down payment deal with seller financing. This would be a "terms" deal.

If you suck at negotiation you will almost always pay too much for the property. You generally make money the day you buy the property. You will likely break even or lose money on a rehab where you have paid too much for the property initially. If you are a wholesaler, your investor buyer will quickly move on to other wholesalers if you send the bad deals.

It's important to get over your fear of negotiation. Almost everyone has this challenge in the beginning.

#5 – Knowing the numbers

You can't make intelligent offers if you don't know your numbers. In order to more thoroughly understand the numbers, you have to understand how much a potential renovation is going to cost. There are no shortcuts when it comes to learning how to estimate repairs. First of all, you need a property inspection form that you use to walk through the house and note anything that needs to be repaired or replaced. Once you have determined what needs to be repaired or replaced, then you have to determine how much that will cost.

When it comes to learning how to estimate repairs, I spent a lot of time in Home Depot when I first got started. You simply must know how much materials cost. How much are cabinets? Then, how much will the installation be? When it comes to the major systems, you can get bids or have contractors give you an estimate on things like the roof, HVAC system, electrical etc. This is one of the benefits of belonging to your local REIA group. You can simply ask someone how much a furnace costs for a 1200 square foot ranch with a basement.

Jeb Brilliant

Primary strategy: Buy & Rehab

Location of investments: Indianapolis, IN, 5 years' experience

Q: Can you describe your investment strategy?

A: At the moment my strategy is to BRRRR houses and apartments, which means I buy them distressed and at a discounted price, I rehab them, and then I either hold it for my own personal portfolio and rent it out or I sell it. I learned many years ago not to pigeon hole myself. When I bought a house to BRRRR but had the opportunity to sell it for a 50% return in almost no time at all with zero risk, I didn't say no because I only wanted to rent it, I pivoted and changed my strategy (so I sold it instead, which makes me technically a flipper as well as buy-and-rehab).

Q: How much time do you typically spend on your investments?

A: I do it full time, but that's about 40 hours/week. Though I'm able to take time off any time I want.

Q: Can you walk us through a typical deal?

A: Generally, my process goes something like:

1. *Begin search for property.* Requires searching through wholesalers. I pretty much only buy from one wholesaler because we have a long history and he takes care of me. It takes little time to look over a bunch of properties but running the numbers and doing background/due diligence on it can take hours. Over time things have changed with my methods as well as the industry. In this day and age, you only have a few hours to a day or so to make a move on a property. Most wholesalers send out their best deals to several of their investors and leave it to the first to send in their earnest money. So, you have to be quick.
2. *Negotiate for property.* Requires back and forth communication with the seller. Because I'm buying from a wholesaler and he's a friend, I try not to negotiate unless the numbers are too close. Then we probably only go back and forth once and I like to do it over the phone versus with text. If negotiation can't be met, back to searching for properties. But for most investors, you would need to negotiate if they need to or can. It's important to try to get the BEST possible price without annoying your team or people.
3. *Close on property.* I ALWAYS do inspections and line up money, which means it's important to know where the money is coming from. I have a hard-money lender I like to use when necessary, or maybe for others it's a HELOC or it could just be cash sitting in a bank account. Requires complete due diligence to be done on property, which includes a property inspection! In my opinion it's SUPER important to do an

inspection in nearly all cases. The ONLY deal I've ever lost money on is the one I didn't follow my checklist and forgot to do an inspection. ALWAYS DO AN INSPECTION!
4. *Begin rehab.* I like to keep rehabs short and quick but sometimes longer ones make you more money. I don't physically swing the hammer, I hire a general contractor (GC) who oversees the contractors. To keep things on track, I keep in touch with my GC and get weekly updates.
5. *Finish investment.* I hold the properties long term, but I usually refinance then hold. Meaning I will refinance the property and pull the money I poured into the property out so I can do it all over again. I always hire a property manager to find tenants for the property, and they continue to manage the property throughout my ownership.

Q: What skills do you use regularly for your strategy?

A: *#1 – Subliminal people skills*

The biggest skill is dealing with people and their nuances. Remembering that general contractors are not always tech-savvy. Allowing people to think I don't know when they're lying to me. For example, I know one guy forgot to call me back, or was just putting it off, but he told me he broke his phone and lost all his text messages. Could be the case, and I let him believe that I believe him.

People like to think they are in control (I won't get into the way people process situations). If they think I believe them, they are likely to keep talking and not clam up. For me communication is one of the most important things. I try to weed out the lies and if they talk long enough they usually get around to the truth in some form or another.

I also get to know people and really listen to them, even if it's them bitching about their kids, spouses, etc. I let them know I'm a working stiff just like them. I do this so we become friends, and I feel like it makes it a little harder for them to want to screw me versus the next asshole investor.

#2 – *Thinking patiently*

One of my mentors saw me react to a situation, and I was about to chew somebody out until he stopped me and told me to slow down and think patiently. This mentor is foreign and at first I thought he mixed some words up, but even if he did he was right. I needed to slow down and process before I acted instead of reacting.

The reason it's important to slow down is because I'm going to make better choices that are better thought out. For example, I've fired property managers before out of sheer reaction, versus a thought out decision, and I've regretted it ever since.

#3 – *Micromanaging*

Micromanaging, or specifically the lack of, is absolutely a skill to perfect. I tend to micromanage and my GCs hate it, so I started asking them for weekly updates and pictures. I still manage what's going on, but I try to let them make the mundane decisions though I've already usually told them what I want, which answers all the questions that come up during a rehab.

It is arduous, but I like to spend a lot of time talking to them about my vision of what a project should look like when it's done. I also hire GC's who invest so I can tell them I want a house done to a standard that will rent for $1,200/month, and we discuss what that is so they can make a decision on crown molding or not by themselves. Though we already had this conversation, so they know what my answer is going to be.

#4 – *Problem solving*

This is probably the single most important skill to have. Pretty much every conversation is about a problem, and it's on the investors shoulders to lead your team to a solution. If it involves another person, I try to put myself in their shoes and understand their side of the situation. If it's a problem with a property then I consider all the options before making a decision. This is NOT easy, but it is necessary to run a business.

#5 – Ability to put out fires

Putting out fires is really just problem-solving, and as a business owner this is what we do on a regular basis. We need to know how to "think patiently" and get through solving problems. A check I sent to my GC overnight hasn't arrived 3 days later, so I'm having to wire the money to him and eat the $30 fee. These are typical fires you have to put out.

#6 – Managing managers

This is key because I'm not the GC, but I treat my GC as a manager and I have to make sure he's always on task.

 # 7 – Asset management

You are your own greatest advocate and so you need to manage your assets. I check on pricing all the time. If I'm told new standard duel-hung double-pained windows are $600 each and I need LOTS of them, I double-check (especially on these big expenses) because I come to find out they really should only be $300 each installed. A good asset manager tries to always preserve capital.

 # 8 – Networking

I'm always networking to grow my business in terms of always looking for more deals, better lenders, potential partners or investors. As much as I may be an antisocial grumpy curmudgeon sometimes, you just have to suck it up and fake it. Go out, shake hands with a smile on your face and pretend you are happy to be there.

Chapter Summary

In this chapter we learnt on Real-Estate Moguls Success Stories:

- Learning from Others
- Sharon Vornholt
- Jeb Brilliant

FINAL WORDS

Becoming a real estate investor is not a destination. It's a journey. On this journey, you'll learn about real estate, how to make money and also about yourself. Be your own biggest encourager. Don't beat yourself up when things don't work out as you planned. Instead, recognize that any challenges that you encounter are all part of the journey. Have fun figuring out how to be a real estate investor. Life's too short to be too serious. Have a sense of humor and laugh along the journey. When things are incredibly good, remember that the highs are part of the ride. When things are not-so-good, keep in mind that the lows are a part of the journey as well.

Real estate investment encompasses a multitude of disciplines and areas of expertise. These include finance, management, development, construction, legal and title, operations, tenancy, investor relations, and capital markets. Even the largest and most successful real estate investment companies have expertise in only some of these areas. Investors must know each property type, the area in which it is located, lease structures, and the intricacies of property operations. As with any business today, the most important asset in a company is the firm's employees, and real estate is no exception. That is why it is critical to have smart, knowledgeable, hardworking, and experienced individuals on the real estate team.

I firmly believe that institutional investors should not commit capital to a private real estate equity firm, unless the senior personnel have gray hair and have been through at least the last two secular downturns. Data analytics will continue to play an increasingly important role in real estate investment and market analysis. As technology evolves and improves, the efficiency of the industry will continue to increase, while operating, and financial costs will continue to decrease. It is viable that within the next twenty years prescriptive data analytics will evolve that will recommend to commercial real estate investors the best property to buy in the best market and with the highest return and lowest risk.

For many, real estate is simple and simple to understand, and investment is easy because it involves a fair exchange between real estate owners (landlords) and real estate users (tenants). As long as the hot water continues to flow and the rent arrives at the right time, everyone is happy. However, real estate investing is more complex because a variety of real estate investments, such as commercial, industrial, residential, are traded on stock exchanges known as REITs. The goal when investing in real estate is to invest in today's jobs and grow and make more money in the future. You need to get enough profit or "return" to cover the risks you take, the taxes you pay and the costs of owning a real estate investment, such as utilities and insurance.

Continually educate yourself while you are taking action. Don't use education as a reason to not get started. Instead, use education to enhance your progress. If you never stop learning more about real estate investing, you'll never stagnate and you'll continue to grow personally and financially.

Believe you can succeed. As Henry Ford said, "Whether you think you can or you think you can't, you're right." Your actions will always follow your beliefs. Believe you can be a real estate investor.

Here's your next step—go take action! Don't be like the majority of

FINAL WORDS

people in this world that allow fear to stop them from pursuing their dreams. Have the courage to step out of your comfort zone and go after the life which you have imagined. This is the first day of the rest of your life. You only live once. Make the most of it. As you can probably tell, I put a tremendous amount of time, effort and passion into writing this book. Although I am a bit biased, I sincerely believe that anyone looking to be a real estate investor should read this book.

Real estate investing is a great way to make money, but it is not for everyone. After reading this book, you should be aware of whether or not rental property investing is the right option for you or if you want to invest in real estate in a different way. Your next step is to invest time in figuring out your real estate market and the potential types of properties available to you. You may find one type of property is better suited to your needs, but also remember that you may have to search for the right location, property, and price. There are benefits, as well as disadvantages of getting into investments in this manner. It is not a magic solution for you to find the right property the first time you go online and look.

As long as you keep your outlook for investing real, then you will succeed. The slow and steady one will win the race to a decent retirement, versus the one that rushes into investing without a proper strategy, funding method, and correct attitude in place. You can get the second vacation home, the dream holiday, or retirement you desire. All you need to do is treat rental property investing like a business and believe in yourself.

The only way to start investing in real estate property is by first understanding the market and everything related to it. The main goal is to be able to understand all the areas of the business. Be able to understand all options available to you since the real estate property market is vast. There are residential, commercials, warehouses, apartments, houses, offices, and many other investment types. By understanding each area and how it works, one can speculate on the risks and returns and anticipate problems before they happen. It will help you make the right

FINAL WORDS

decisions before deciding to settle on a certain area in rental property investment.

Real estate is the only investment where value increases consistently and is not affected significantly by short-term fluctuations. Not only is it 99% risk-free, but you can also make a fortune from the industry. All you need is to uncover the right strategies for a successful investment. Discover how to turn your life around and become a renowned real-estate mogul.

So, enjoy the journey!

Image Credit: Shutterstock.com

www.ingramcontent.com/pod-product-compliance
Lightning Source LLC
Chambersburg PA
CBHW020910080526
44589CB00011B/526